Classic British
Steam Trains

Colin Garratt (author) Thirty years ago, Colin Garratt abandoned a promising commercial career to document, on colour film, the last steam locomotives of the world. This unique odyssey – which continues apace – has taken him to more than fifty countries and some of the remotest places on earth. Colin has written and illustrated over fifty books on railways, travel and photography, including his autobiography, and he is also widely known for his work in radio and television. Colin Garratt is the Director of Milepost 92½ – picture library and photographers to the railway industry.

With special thanks to Roger Crombleholme for assistance with the captions.

All pictures provided by Milepost 92½ (www.railphotolibrary.com)

Publisher and Creative Director Nick Wells
Senior Editor Sarah Goulding
Designer Lucy Robins

This is a **STAR FIRE** book

STAR FIRE BOOKS
Crabtree Hall, Crabtree Lane
Fulham, London SW6 6TY

www.star-fire.co.uk

Star Fire is part of The Foundry Creative Media Company Limited

First published in 2006

Copyright © 2006 The Foundry

05 07 09 08 06
1 3 5 7 9 10 8 6 4 2

A CIP record for this book is available from the British Library.

ISBN 1 84451 460 9

Printed in China

Classic British
Steam Trains

STAR
FIRE

CONTENTS

$\mathscr{I}$NTRODUCTION

British steam locomotive development in the 20th century was both innovative and dramatic. The excitement to come was anticipated in the amazing 'railway races' between London and Aberdeen in 1895, when the east and west coast routes vied for supremacy. Amid this intense inter-company rivalry, small locomotives were pushed to incredible limits: Aberdeen was reached in 8 hours and 40 minutes and, as part of the action, the London and North Western Railway's Webb Precedent 2-4-0 'Hardwicke' ran the 141 miles between Crewe and Carlisle at an average speed of 67.2 mph.

The beginning of the 20th century saw the Great Western Railway's 4-4-0 'City of Truro' achieve a speed of 102.3 mph on the descent of Wellington Bank in Somerset – the first time any manmade creation had reached a three figure speed. The evolution of the steam locomotive was dominated by two factors: the quest for more speed and more power. Accordingly, the new century saw the beautiful inside cylinder 4-4-0s, which worked many expresses of the late Victorian period, give way to the Atlantic 4-4-2 and the 4-6-0. By the 1920s the Pacific 4-6-2 had been introduced, and this form of locomotive was destined to be Britain's ultimate express passenger type.

The '1923 Grouping' saw Britain's numerous private railway companies merged to create the 'Big Four': the London and North Eastern Railway (L.N.E.R.), the London, Midland and Scottish Railway (L.M.S.), the Great Western Railway (G.W.R.) and the Southern Railway (S.R.). But this did little to stem rivalry, especially between the east and west coast routes of the L.N.E.R. and L.M.S. respectively, and in 1937 the L.M.S. Pacific 'Coronation' reached 114 mph down Madely Bank between Stafford and Crewe. However, the L.N.E.R. ensured that this triumph was short lived, and the following year the Gresley A4 Pacific 'Mallard' achieved 126 mph down Stoke Bank between Grantham and Peterborough – a world record for steam traction which stands to this day. Neither, incidentally, has the record ever been beaten by a conventional diesel locomotive.

The heyday of the Pacific coincided with the advent of streamlining, which added a flamboyance to the locomotive that was fully exploited by the publicity departments of the railways concerned. The last streamliners built were Bulleid's 'Merchant

Navies' of 1941 and his 'Light Pacifics' – the West Countries and Battle of Britains – in 1945.

Freight train operation at the beginning of the 20th century was largely in the hands of inside cylinder 0-6-0s, a form of engine first introduced in the 1830s, with building continuing until the 1940s with dozens of different designs which were little more than variations on a theme. The 0-8-0 was a logical development, but it flourished on relatively few railways. The 2-8-0 first appeared on the Great Western in 1903 and this form of locomotive was to remain prevalent as a main line freight hauler until the end of steam. The 2-8-2 Mikado only occurred in Gresley's L.N.E.R. P1s and P2s, but only a few were built whilst the Garratt type only manifested in Gresley's solitary U1 2-8-2+2-8-2 and the 32 L.M.S. Garratts of 1927. The 2-8-0 really came into its own with Stanier's 8Fs of 1935 and the members of this class were increased dramatically during World War II. The 8Fs also formed the basis for the United States Army Transportation Corps S160s and the British War Department 2-8-0s. These three types alone reached a total of some 4,000 locomotives.

Branch line and suburban workings were invariably in the hands of tank engines, although many down-graded tender engines lived out their twilight years on branch or secondary routes. The 20th century also saw the concept of the mixed traffic locomotive develop – engines equally suitable for freight or passenger work – personified by such types as the L.M.S. 'Black 5' 4-6-0s, the Great Western 'Hall' 4-6-0s and L.N.E.R.

B1 4-6-0s, although the first numerous mixed traffic type was Ramsbottom's DX 0-6-0s. These 'maids of all work' reached a total of 943 engines.

Shunting engines were invariably six-coupled tanks characterised by the L.M.S. 'Jinties' or the Great Western 57XX pannier tanks, of which 863 were put into operation. However the development of shunting engines proper was limited, as many former main line freight engines eked out their days in the shunting yards. Diesels also made early incursions into this work with examples appearing on the LMS as early as the 1930s.

In 1948, Britain's railways were nationalised, which led to the introduction of the 12 standard types intended to replace the plethora of designs inherited not only from the 'Big Four', but also the pre-grouping companies as well. The first type produced were the 'Britannias'. These mixed traffic Pacifics were followed by the Standard 5, 4-6-0s based closely on the design of the 'Black 5' of some twenty years earlier. Smaller standard designs were meant to fulfil a wide range of secondary duties. All the standards were designated mixed traffic except for the 9F 2-10-0s, which were designated as heavy mineral engines. In the event the 9Fs proved to be excellent mixed traffic engines, even capable of working heavy main line expresses at speeds in the 70s. However, this practice was eventually forbidden and the 9Fs resorted to their original role. No sooner had the production of the standards got underway than the government announced the Railway Modernisation Plan, under which steam traction was to be phased out. This meant that the standards were destined to go to the scrapyard not only prematurely, but alongside the very classes they had been intended to replace.

The rundown of steam traction in the 1960s was paralleled by the disastrous Beeching Plan when, under a Conservative government, Richard Beeching from ICI was given the brief to make the railways pay in the face of the rampant and uncontrolled proliferation of road transport. His answer was to close down a third of the railway network.

To a nation of railway lovers, the phasing out of steam traction was a disaster. The government had earmarked a small selection of locomotives to be stuffed and mounted in a museum as testimony to the age of steam, but a million railway enthusiasts protested and the railway preservation movement was born. Hundreds of locomotives were rescued from scrapyards. In addition, Beeching had left a mass of closed lines, many in picturesque areas with enormous tourist potential, and the preservationists took over many of these lines which have now become internationally well known. Volunteer labour was essential from the outset and to a large extent still is, notwithstanding the enormous popularity of these railways.

Beyond the main line railway, Britain had many thousands of small industrial locomotives which operated in collieries, iron and steel works, quarries, docks and a vast range of manufactories ranging from paper mills to biscuit factories. Some of these engines outlived their main line relations by upwards of 15 years, and so were a ready target for the preservationists. Today, many of these industrial engines can be seen on preserved lines hauling passenger trains – an unimaginable concept at the time of their building.

Britain's indigenous railways are just a part of the story of steam, as Britain was the railway builder to an empire and the world. Thousands of locomotives were built in foundries set in the industrial heartland of Britain and rolled onto the deck of ships for export to all areas of the world. Many of these foundries are now legendary names in industrial folklore.

Predictably, many exported locomotives were built in the classic British style, and engines whose spiritual home lay in the soft English countryside could be seen toiling across the plains of India or the pampas of Argentina. However, many of the latter day exports were types that found little or no favour in the mother country, such as 2-8-2, 2-8-4, 4-8-0 and 4-8-2, along with Kitson Meyer Mallets and Garratts. Some exported British-built locomotives outlived their indigenous relations by up to 25 years, and a few have even been repatriated and can be seen at work on preserved lines, such as the first exported Garratt which went to Tasmania. The last exported British steam locomotive, in the form of an 0-4-2ST built by Hunslet of Leeds in 1971, has also been returned from a sugar mill in Java.

The steam locomotive has, since its inception, fascinated young and old alike, and nowhere on earth has a love of steam trains been more prevalent than in Britain. It was the one truly living machine and ran on the raw elements of fire and water; it was the motive force of the Industrial Revolution; it was a particularly sensual, beautiful and awe-inspiring creation. It will never die, and will continue to fascinate for years to come. The history of railways will be studied by future generations and the evolution of the steam locomotive will be a particularly inspiring aspect, for it was arguably Britain's greatest technological gift to mankind.

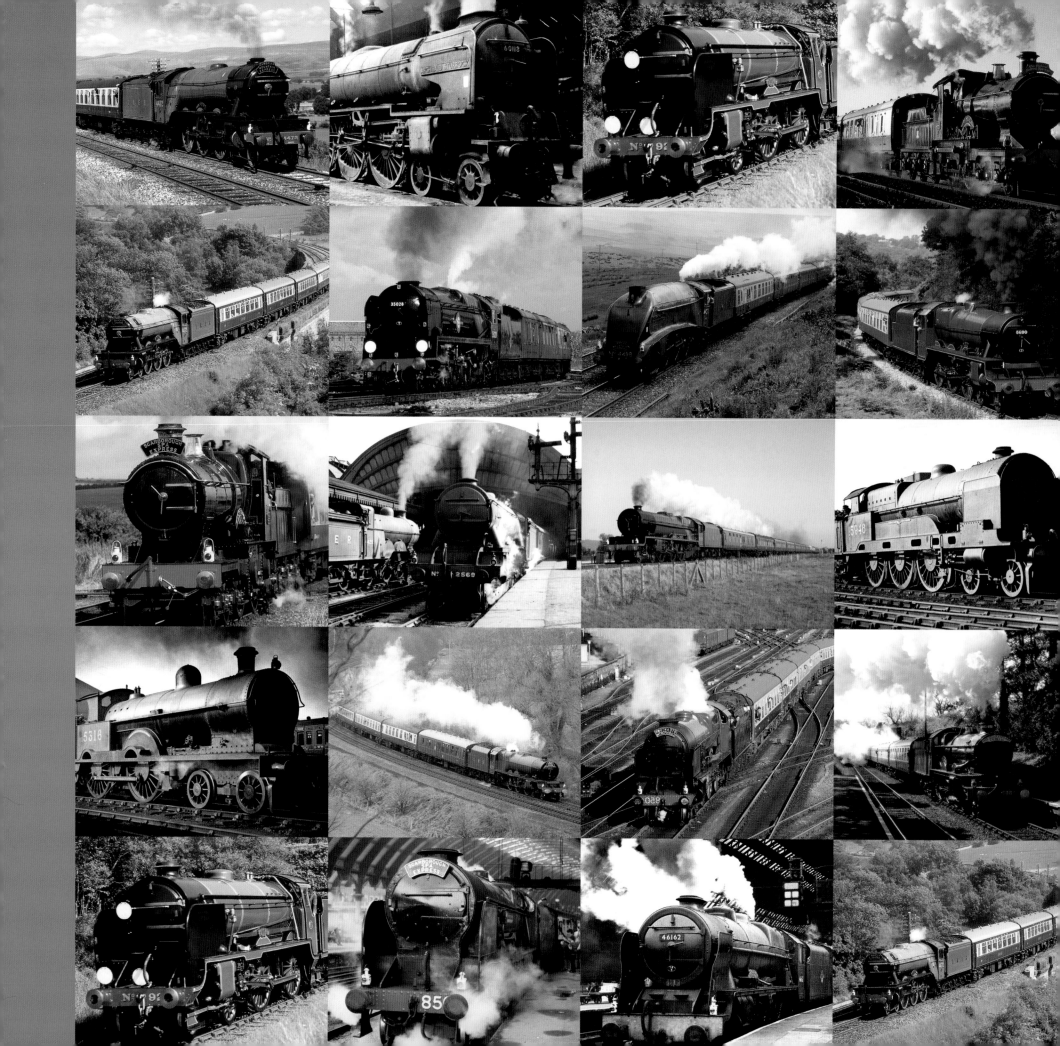

PASSENGER TRAINS

To many people, passenger trains are the railway. Exciting and heroic names such as 'The Flying Scotsman', 'The Cornish Riviera Express', 'The Golden Arrow' and 'The Royal Scot' conjure up visions of high profile, fast, luxurious travel.

These trains are the stuff of legend and romance; the stuff of the great races to the north between the L.M.S. and the L.N.E.R.; of the Great Western's 'City of Truro' becoming the first steam locomotive to achieve a speed in excess of 100 mph; and of 'The Orient Express' taking the rich and famous from London to Dover to catch the ferry and then onwards by train again across the continent to exotic destinations such as Vence and Istanbul.

The engines that hauled these trains were a highly specialised breed. They were designed with large wheels, which were necessary to keep the moving parts running at moderate speeds. Beginning with the Singles, typified by Patrick Stirling's No. 1 for the Great Northen Railway, the genre gravitated, by the end of the nineteenth century, to 2-4-0s and 4-4-0s and reached its ultimate development with the Pacific 4-6-2, the most famous example of which is undoubtedly the record breaking 'Mallard'.

L.M.S. 'JUBILEE' 5XP

4-6-0

The L.M.S. 'Jubilee' 4-6-0s were conceived by William Stanier as a taper boiler development of the existing 'Patriot' class, and 79 engines were ordered straight off the drawing board in 1934. Initially poor steaming compromised their performance, however, and it took three years to find a cure. Once remedied, the 'Jubilees' were transformed and performed superbly on the former Midland main lines from London to Manchester and over the Settle and Carlisle route. In all, 191 engines were built and it was not until 1967 that the final three were retired from the Leeds Holbeck shed.

S.R. 'SCHOOLS'
4-4-0

The constricted loading gauge of the Tonbridge–Hastings line had always imposed severe restrictions on locomotive design, ruling out the larger classes that its train loadings called for. Richard Maunsell's masterpiece, the 'Schools' or 'V' class 4-4-0 of 1930, was tailored to the requirements of the route. With three cylinders powering four coupled wheels, it had all the power needed within a short frame length, and its angled-in profile fitted within the width restrictions of the tunnels. In all, 40 were built and named after famous private and public schools.

L.N.E.R. A1
4-6-2

Thompson's rebuilding of Gresley's pioneer Pacific No. 4470 'Great Northern' in 1945 was intended to produce the prototype of a new class of 4-6-2s, but it was an ungainly and uninspiring machine. However, his successor, Arthur Peppercorn, radically changed the design and produced one of the finest British express locomotives, fittingly classified A1. The first of the class emerged from Doncaster works after Nationalisation in August 1948. In addition to their reputation for fast running, the A1s were extremely reliable and ran considerable mileages between overhauls. All 49 were scrapped in 1966, but a fiftieth member of the class, No. 60163 'Tornado', is currently under construction at Darlington.

S.R. 'LORD NELSON'
4-6-0

Soon after its formation, the Southern Railway foresaw the need for an express passenger locomotive capable of working 500-tonne trains at a 55 mph average. In 1926, Richard Maunsell produced the engine that answered these requirements. No. 850 'Lord Nelson' was a four-cylinder 4-6-0, designed to meet the prevailing 21-tonne axle loading. After thorough trials with the prototype, fifteen more emerged from Eastleigh works in 1928–29, all named after famous sea lords and admirals. They worked initially on the Continental expresses between Victoria and Dover, though in the postwar years they were principally used on Southampton boat trains.

G.N.R. STIRLING SINGLE

Patrick Stirling's eight-foot Singles were a supreme example of engineering artistry, although they departed from his normal practice by incorporating both a leading bogie and outside cylinders. No. 1, the first of these celebrated and graceful locomotives, was built at Doncaster in 1870 and no fewer than 53 were built over a period of 25 years. For much of this time they hauled the fastest G.N.R. expresses from King's Cross, whilst two of the class distinguished themselves in the 1888 and 1895 races to the North. Fittingly, the original No. 1 has been preserved and was returned to steam in 1981.

L.M.S. REBUILT 'ROYAL SCOT'

4-6-0

The entry into service in 1927 of the first 50 'Royal Scots' at last gave the L.M.S. a worthy express passenger locomotive. Twenty more came from Derby works in 1930. An additional locomotive was built with an experimental super-pressure boiler, but suffered a fatal tube burst whilst on trial. Stanier fitted its chassis with a large taper boiler with double blastpipe and chimney to form the prototype for rebuilding the rest of the class. It was a process that took until 1955 to complete, but it transformed good engines into excellent ones. The rebuilt 'Scots' delivered the highest power output per tonne of any British 4-6-0, outclassing even the G.W.R. 'Kings'.

L.N.E.R. A3

4-6-2

The first two Gresley Pacifics appeared on the Great Northern Railway in 1922, creating a sensation due to their size and sleek, modern lines. By the time Doncaster works delivered the next ten production engines, the G.N.R. had been absorbed into the L.N.E.R. This company arranged a Locomotive Exchange trial with the G.W.R. in 1925 in which the Great Western 'Castle' outshone the performances of the Pacifics, and did it on ten per cent less coal. Gresley promptly redesigned his Pacifics to incorporate the long-travel valves and higher boiler pressure of the G.W.R. and the revised engines, classified A3, were a revelation in speed and fuel economy.

G.W.R. 'CITY'

4-4-0

In the transition from Dean to Churchward on the G.W.R., several of the traditional Great Western double-framed 4-4-0s were rebuilt, with the American-inspired taper boiler allied to the Belgian Belpaire firebox which was to become the hallmark of Churchward's designs. Ten new express 4-4-0s of similar appearance were ordered from Swindon works in 1903 and named after cities served by the G.W.R. They quickly proved to be exceedingly fast machines and recorded many high speed runs, but their lasting fame is down to No. 3440 'City of Truro', which raced down Wellington bank in Somerset on 9th May 1904 at the head of the 'Ocean Mails Express' and was unofficially timed at 102.3 mph.

L.M.S. 'PRINCESS CORONATION'

4-6-2 (Non-streamlined)

After the first ten streamlined L.M.S. Pacifics had entered service, a further five were outshopped in non-streamlined form, revealing the handsome and powerful profile that lay beneath the casing. On a test run in February 1939, No. 6234 'Duchess of Abercorn' showed just how powerful they were. Hauling a 20-coach, 605-tonne train from Crewe to Glasgow and back, she recorded an indicated horsepower of 3,330 whilst climbing Beattock bank, a power output from a steam locomotive that has never been matched in Britain. All the streamliners lost their casings after the war but three of these magnificent machines have been preserved.

L.N.E.R. A3

4-6-2

Arguably the most famous locomotive in the world, No. 4472 'Flying Scotsman' was the first Pacific to be built by the L.N.E.R. in 1923. The locomotive hauled the 10 am from King's Cross – the famous 'Flying Scotsman' – on its inaugural run of 392 miles to Edinburgh in 1928, the longest non-stop journey in the world. The same engine hit the headlines again in 1934 by achieving the first authenticated 100 mph by a steam locomotive. Small wonder that when it was retired from King's Cross shed in 1963, it was purchased for preservation and has since led an eventful life, travelling the world.

L.N.E.R. A3

4-6-2

All the L.N.E.R. Gresley Pacifics were uprated with new boilers and piston valves after 1925, and most of the class were named after famous racehorses. In 1935, No. 2750 'Papyrus' touched 108 mph on a high-speed trial between London and Newcastle, which remains the world record for a non-streamlined locomotive. Although joined by later Pacifics after World War II, the A3s remained the mainstay of east coast express passenger services. In 1957 they were given a new lease of life by the fitting of Kylchap double blastpipes and chimneys, and they were subsequently given German-style smoke deflectors.

L.M.S. REBUILT 'CLAUGHTON'

4-6-0

Bowen-Cooke's four-cylinder 4-6-0s of 1913 were the largest express engines built for the L.N.W.R. The first was named 'Sir Gilbert Claughton' and ultimately 130 were constructed up to 1921. They were somewhat underboilered in relation to their cylinder capacity, so in 1928 twenty of them were given much bigger boilers, and some engines were fitted with Beardmore-Caprotti valve gear. In this form they performed with great gusto but withdrawals during the 1930s left a solitary example, No. 6004, surviving long enough to become British Rail property in 1948.

S.R. 'MERCHANT NAVY'

4-6-2

Bulleid's Pacifics in their original form were some of the most remarkable machines ever seen on rails. In many ways they were outstanding – their welded high-pressure boilers were the finest steam-raisers ever fitted to a British locomotive. But in other respects they were impossibly troublesome. The chain-driven valve gear operating within a totally enclosed oil bath was fine in theory, but in service the casings leaked, allowing oil out and water in. All 30 'Merchant Navy' Pacifics were comprehensively rebuilt between 1956 and 1959, having their 'air-smoothed' casings removed and the problematic valve gear replaced by the Walschaerts variety.

G.W.R. 'KING'

4-6-0

The 'Kings' represented the ultimate development in size of the G.W.R. four-cylinder 4-6-0, being in every respect an enlargement of the 'Castle'. To accommodate it, track improvements and bridge strengthening had to be undertaken on the main line, but even then, the 'Kings' were confined to the Paddington to Plymouth and Wolverhampton routes. No. 6000 'King George V' entered service in June 1927, and within a few weeks was shipped to the USA to take part in the Baltimore & Ohio Railroad's centenary celebrations. The Americans awarded it the bell that it still carries on its front footplating.

L.N.W.R. 'PRECURSOR'
4-4-0

When George Whale succeeded F. W. Webb at Crewe in 1903, his first task was to provide the L.N.W.R. with a powerful and reliable express passenger locomotive to replace Webb's dismal compounds. No. 513 'Precursor', which emerged from Crewe in 1904, proved to be the answer – a simple robust 4-4-0 that could tackle the loads of the day without the need for piloting. The class was quickly multiplied, no less than 110 of them being constructed at Crewe over the next two years. Another 20 were built in 1907, and for several years they bore the brunt of handling the L.N.W.R.'s main line trains.

L.N.E.R. A4
4-6-2

The A4 class streamlined Pacifics introduced by Sir Nigel Gresley in 1935 achieved instant and sensational success in high-speed running. The pioneer engine, No. 2509 'Silver Link', attained a speed of 112.5 mph within a few weeks of entering service at the head of the 'Silver Jubilee' express service to Newcastle, and in 1938 No. 4468 'Mallard' attained the world speed record for steam, 126 mph. 'Mallard' was the first A4 to benefit from a Kylchap double blastpipe and chimney, with which the whole class were subsequently equipped.

G.W.R. 'CITY'
4-4-0

Though the G.W.R. 'Cities' were assured a lasting place in railway history, their working lives were comparatively short, being displaced from express work by Churchward and Collett's larger 4-6-0s. They were moved to work on secondary routes, but withdrawals began after just 24 years of service. By 1931, only two remained, 'City of Truro' being one of them. Its survival is to the credit of the L.N.E.R., who offered to display the engine in the National Railway Museum, York. Since that time, it has been restored to working order and has visited several preserved railways.

S.R. 'LORD NELSON'
4-6-0

A peculiarity of the 'Lord Nelsons' lay in the setting of the crank angles by which the engine gave eight exhausts per revolution of the driving wheels instead of four, resulting in a very soft blast and even torque. They required skilful firing to give the best performance but were enormously improved by Oliver Bulleid, who fitted the class with the Lemaitre five-jet multiple blastpipe and larger piston valves. The class worked until 1962, when happily No. 30850 'Lord Nelson' was selected for preservation in the National Collection.

G.N.R. ATLANTIC &
L.N.E.R. PACIFIC

At the time of their introduction in 1902, the large-boilered Great Northern Atlantics made an immediate visual impact appropriate for what was then the largest passenger engine in the country. When later fitted with a superheater, the Ivatt Atlantic became a very fine engine indeed, and made a more than capable stablemate for Gresley's much larger Pacifics. Atlantic No. 4425 rests between duties at York as A3 No. 2569 'Gladiateur' makes an imperious start with a southbound express.

G.W.R. 'SAINT'

4-6-0

After the flowing lines of William Dean's double-framed 4-4-0s, the starkly modernistic appearance of Churchward's first 4-6-0 of 1902 came as a culture shock to Swindon-watchers. It was an outside-cylinder locomotive with a high-pitched domeless boiler that seemed to echo contemporary American practice. In 1905, further engines of similar outline appeared, several of them running as 4-4-2s for comparison, but all were eventually converted to 4-6-0s. The main production batch followed in 1906, and the whole class was named after 'Saints', 'Ladies' and 'Courts'.

L.M.S. 'PRINCESS ROYAL'

4-6-2

When William Stanier was appointed to the L.M.S. in 1932, the 'Royal Scot' 4-6-0s were being pushed to their limits handling the company's principal London–Glasgow services. He concluded that a much larger machine was needed to haul 500-tonne trains the entire 400 miles without the need for changing engines at Carlisle. Drawing on his Swindon experience, he took as the basis for his new Pacific the dimensions and chassis layout of the G.W.R. 'King' class 4-6-0, extending the frames at the rear with a trailing truck to support a much larger boiler with a wide firebox. In effect, he created a much enlarged and modernised version of the G.W.R.'s 1908 Pacific, 'The Great Bear'.

L.M.S. STREAMLINED 'PRINCESS CORONATION'

4-6-2

Spurred on by the records set by the L.N.E.R.'s high-speed streamlined services, the L.M.S. responded in July 1937 by introducing the 'Coronation Scot' service, maintaining a regular six hour London to Glasgow schedule. Simultaneously, William Stanier produced his finest design, the 'Princess Coronation' four-cylinder Pacifics. The first five entered service with stylish blue and silver streamlined casings to match the new trains, and soon showed their prodigious power and speed. On a special run from Euston to Crewe in 1937, No. 6220 'Coronation' set a new British speed record of 114 mph.

L.M.S. 'PRINCESS ROYAL'

4-6-2

The first two 'Princess Royal' Pacifics emerged from Crewe works in 1933 and fulfilled their designer's expectations. No. 6201 'Princess Elizabeth' set an impressive record in 1936, hauling a seven coach train non-stop from London to Glasgow in under six hours, an unprecedented feat. Fittingly, this locomotive has been preserved, together with the first of the production batch, No. 6203 'Princess Margaret Rose', and both have been active on main line excursions in recent years.

G.W.R. 'CASTLE'

4-6-0

Unlike Churchward, Charles Collett was not a groundbreaking engineer, choosing instead to build steadily on his predecessor's designs within the G.W.R. tradition. His 'Castle' class of 1923 is a case in point, being a larger and more powerful version of Churchward's four-cylinder 'Star' class of 1906. This was achieved by fitting a bigger boiler and cylinders to the 'Star' chassis, producing a locomotive that was to become the G.W.R.'s principal express type for the next 35 years. 171 locomotives were constructed in total, including several rebuilt from 'Stars', the final 'Castle' emerging from Swindon in 1950.

FREIGHT TRAINS

It is sometimes forgotten that the railways were moving freight before they were moving passengers. Steam locomotives were a development of industrial stationary steam engines, and when Richard Trevithick constructed his 1804 locomotive, it was to transport raw material from the Penydarren ironworks near Merthyr Tydfil. Many of the early locomotive developments came from the need to move heavy minerals to fuel the Industrial Revolution.

Since its inception, the railway has always been the natural carrier for heavy, bulky loads which need to be transported over great distances, replacing the earlier method of transporting such materials by canal. As the rail network grew to cover the country, so its popularity as a carrier of freight grew. Soon every sort of commodity was being carried by rail, and specialised rolling stock was developed to allow the transportation of perishables such as fruit, vegetables and meat.

The main line freight locomotive evolved in 1825, when 'Locomotion' was used on the Stockton and Darlington Railway. Freight haulers were, by definition, tender engines which were either 0-6-0s or 0-8-0s in their formative years, and developed to the 9F 2-10-0 at the end of steam on British Rail. Most were characterised by small wheels designed to provide maximum adhesion when starting heavy loads.

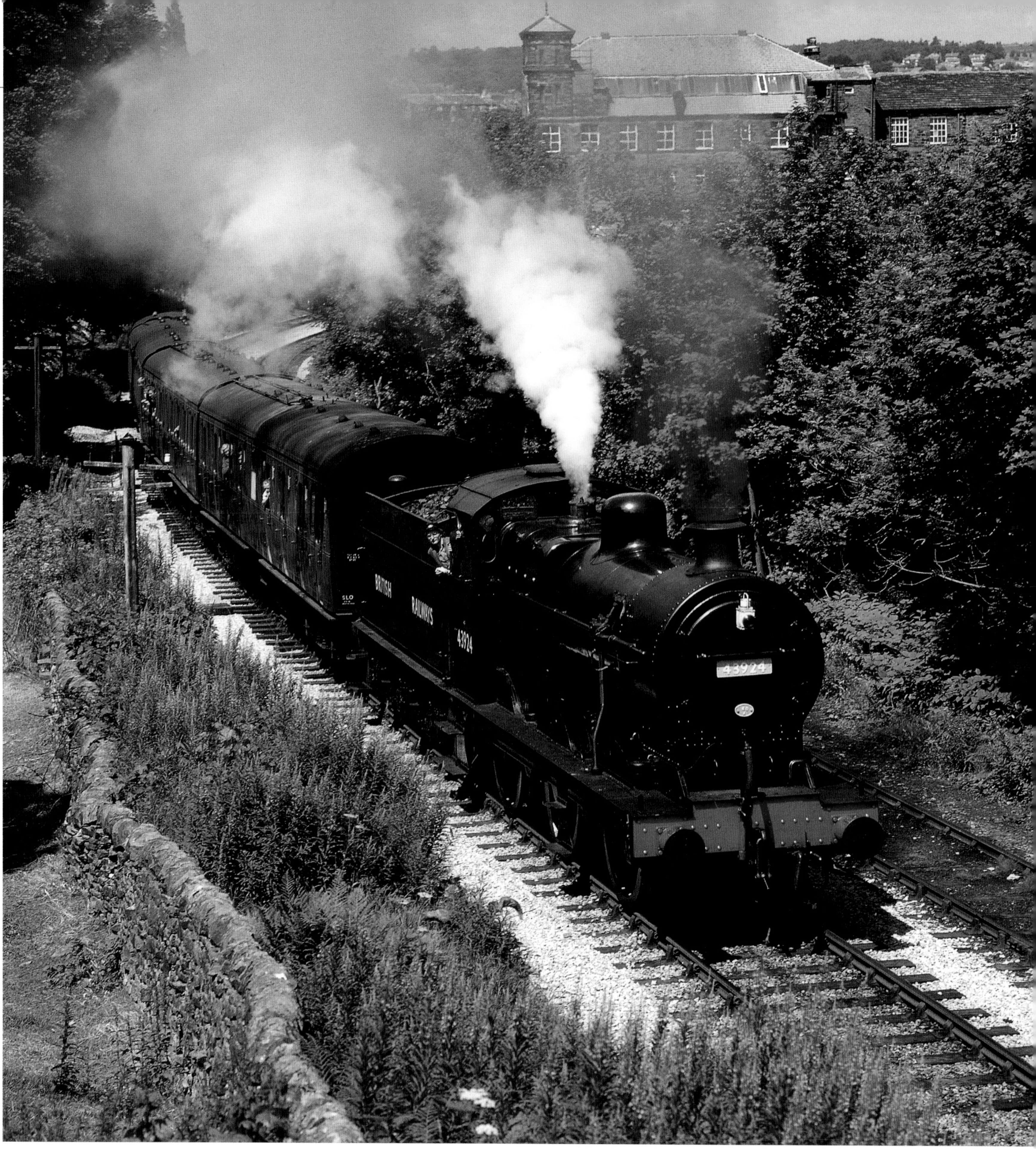
BRITISH RAILWAYS
43924
43924

MIDLAND RAILWAY 4F

0-6-0

The six-coupled goods engine remained the mainstay of Midland Railway freight haulage throughout its existence, and the largest examples of the type were Henry Fowler's Class 4 locomotives introduced in 1911. They enlarged and uprated the earlier Johnson and Deeley designs and were equipped with superheaters. Inevitably, however, they were fitted with undersized axlebox bearings, that Achilles heel of Midland locomotives. Volume production began in 1917 and continued steadily until the Grouping in 1923, when 197 were at work.

B.R. 9F

2-10-0

The 9F 2-10-0 was easily the most successful of the B.R. Standard classes. Yet its entry into service coincided with the Modernisation Plan that would render the engines obsolete with the end of steam traction. The design was to have been a 2-8-2, but encouraged by the success of his 'Austerity' 2-10-0s, Robert Riddles decided on a ten-coupled chassis. The first 9Fs to emerge from Crewe were allocated to the heavy iron ore workings in south Wales and County Durham, immediately showing themselves masters of these duties. But, most surprisingly, when they were tried on passenger trains, their 5 ft (1.6 m) diameter driving wheels proved no obstacle to running at speeds of up to 90 mph.

N.B.R. J36

0-6-0

Matthew Holmes' C class 0-6-0 was the most numerous class on the North British Railway. Construction began at Cowlairs works in 1888, and 168 engines were in traffic by 1900. As built, they were under-boilered and offered scant protection for the crew, but were later rebuilt with larger boilers and side-window cabs. It was in this form that 25 of the class were requisitioned for service on the Western Front during World War I. In recognition of their wartime work, these engines were named after places and personalities associated with the conflict. Most of the class became B.R. property, and by 1967 two of them had become the last working steam locomotives in Scotland.

N.E.R. Q6

0-8-0

Raven's T2 120-strong class of 0-8-0s was introduced on the N.E.R. in 1913 for working heavy coal traffic. Powerful engines, built with superheated boilers and steam reversing gear, they were popular with footplate crews all over the North East. The last survivors were withdrawn in 1967 and sold for scrap, but a determined effort by enthusiasts raised enough money to buy No. 63395 (N.E.R. No. 2238) from a scrap dealer in Blyth. The engine was moved to the North Yorkshire Moors Railway where it has been vacuum-fitted and returned to working order.

B.R. 9F

2-10-0

Construction of the B.R. Standard 9Fs ceased in March 1960 with the delivery of No. 92220 from Swindon works. As the final steam locomotive built for B.R., it was honoured with the name 'Evening Star'. Just four years later, the first of the 251-strong class went to the scrapyard, despite being good for another 20 years' work. Within three years the class was extinct and 'Evening Star' was set aside for the National Collection, to be joined in preservation by eight further examples rescued from the scrap lines.

L.M.S. 8F

2-8-0

Right from its formation in 1923, the L.M.S. struggled to equip itself with a modern heavy goods locomotive. Throughout the 1920s it depended on ageing 0-8-0s and underpowered 0-6-0s to handle its considerable volume of freight traffic. Even the 33 Beyer-Garratts in 1927 had unredeemable faults, so it was only after the arrival of William Stanier in 1932 that the right locomotive for the job was born. Stanier's solution was an eight-coupled design derived from Churchward's G.W.R. 28XX class and incorporating the best features of the highly successful 'Black 5s'.

S.R. Q1

0-6-0

Always willing to take an unconventional approach to locomotive design, Oliver Bulleid's challenge in 1942 was to produce a light yet powerful six-coupled goods engine for the Southern Railway. Wartime shortages meant a need to save on materials as well as weight, so out went the running plate and splashers and in came 'boxpok' wheels. The horseshoe shape of the boiler was dictated by the use of a new type of lagging material, and welding was extensively used instead of castings. The result may have looked extraordinary but the Q1 was the most powerful British 0-6-0 ever built. Forty engines were built in 1942 and the class remained intact for the next 21 years.

G.C.R. O4

2-8-0

The first of John Robinson's 8K class 2-8-0s emerged from Gorton works in 1911, in anticipation of increased traffic from the G.C.R.'s vast new docks complex at Immingham. By June 1914, 126 were in traffic. Two years later, the design was adopted by the Ministry of Munitions for wartime service and massive orders for more locomotives were divided between Gorton and outside builders. Over 500 more of the type were produced, though many never ventured overseas as intended and all the government engines became available for disposal at the end of the war. The majority were bought by the G.W.R., L.N.W.R. and by the L.N.E.R., who classified them class O4.

MIDLAND RAILWAY 4F

0-6-0

The prevailing Midland influence within the newly-formed L.M.S. ensured that the Class 4 was adopted as the standard freight loco. More and more were built every year up to 1928 and there was even a final batch of 45 outshopped in 1937, taking the class total to 772. Remarkably, nothing was ever done to rectify their design shortcomings. All entered B.R. stock at Nationalisation and the last was not retired until 1966. Four have been preserved, including No. 4027, the first L.M.S.-built 4F of 1923.

N.E.R. J27
0-6-0

The North Eastern Railway relied for its prosperity on mineral traffic and always maintained a high proportion of goods engines in its fleet. Sir Vincent Raven's P3 class 0-6-0s of 1906 were the ultimate development of earlier Worsdell classes, and were rugged, reliable machines. Construction continued right to the end of the N.E.R.'s separate existence until 115 locomotives were in service, the later engines being superheated and fitted with piston valves. The final member of the class, N.E.R. No. 2392 (B.R. No. 65894) was the last N.E.R. engine built before the Grouping and, fittingly, is the preserved example of the class, residing on the North Yorkshire Moors Railway.

G.W.R. 42XX/5205
2-8-0T

The first 42XX 2-8-0T emerged from Swindon in 1910 as a tank engine version of Churchward's successful 28XX class 2-8-0s. By 1923, no fewer than 104 had been built to handle the G.W.R.'s short-haul mineral traffic. Collett then brought out a slightly enlarged version, the 5205 class, and these appeared in batches throughout the 1920s. But the economic depression had dramatically reduced the south Wales coal traffic by 1930, so the next 20 engines were stored before being rebuilt with enlarged coal bunker, extended frames and a trailing axle to become the 72XX class 2-8-2T. A further 34 conversions to 2-8-2Ts followed, but wartime demands exposed a shortage of 2-8-0Ts, so ten new 5205 class tanks were quickly constructed in 1940.

L.M.S. 8F & 4F AT PEAK FOREST

2-8-0

In wartime Britain, the demand for heavy freight engines meant that Stanier 8Fs were built under government contracts by the G.W.R., L.N.E.R. and Southern workshops and so were used on all the 'Big Four' railways. Once Class 8 motive power became available for heavy freight haulage, the L.M.S. was able to reallocate its stock of 4F 0-6-0s to lesser duties. The changeover is captured perfectly by 8F 48605 bringing a lengthy rake of limestone empties through Peak Forest station, whilst the driver of 4F 43950 relaxes before taking out a local goods train.

S.E. & C.R. C

0-6-0

The first of Harry Wainwright's 108-strong C class 0-6-0s appeared in 1900. They were robustly built and elegant in appearance, particularly when attired in full Wainwright livery, one of the most ornate and beautiful ever seen in Britain. The C class served the S.E. & C.R. and the Southern Railway reliably, and handled branch line passenger trains as well as goods. All but three were still in service at Nationalisation and the last survivor, No. 592, which ended its days as Ashford works shunter, is preserved on the Bluebell Railway.

L.M.S. 8F

2-8-0

Following Nationalisation, all British-based 8Fs were taken into London Midland Region stock and were joined by 39 engines returned from overseas until the B.R.'s total reached 666. Many of the 2-8-0s, however, remained abroad and worked on throughout the Middle East and in Italy. Some Turkish-based 8Fs could even be found at work until the 1980s. At home, around 150 survived into the last year of B.R. steam, 1968, hard at work to the very end. Seven of these have been preserved and an eighth locomotive has been repatriated from Turkey.

L.M.S. GARRATT

2-8-0

For the first decade of its existence, the L.M.S. suffered from the perpetuation of the Midland Railway's small engine policy, resulting in the regular double-heading of heavy freight trains by pairs of 0-6-0 tender engines. To remedy this, the management turned to Beyer Peacocks and ordered 33 Garratts, but unfortunately Midland thinking insisted that they had to be the equivalent of two 4F 0-6-0s in all their leading dimensions. They were inherently unsuited to fast running, due to poor valve events and typically-Midland undersized bearings. As soon as the B.R. Standard 9Fs were in traffic, the Garratts were swiftly withdrawn.

SOMERSET & DORSET

2-8-0

The S. & D.J.R. was jointly owned by the Midland and the London South Western Railways, with the former being responsible for locomotives and rolling stock. These powerful 2-8-0s introduced in 1914 by Sir Henry Fowler broke with the Midland 'small engine' tradition, but were just what was needed to take heavy mineral trains over the Mendips unaided. Strangely enough, the Midland never built anything larger than an 0-6-0 for its own heavy freight traffic. Six engines came from Derby in 1914, followed by a further five from Stephensons in 1925. Withdrawals started in 1959 following the arrival of the B.R. 9F 2-10-0s, but two of the 1925 locomotives have survived.

G.W.R. 28XX

2-8-0

With the South Wales mineral traffic in mind, Churchward embarked on the design of his heavy freight engine of 1903, inspired by American experience of the 2-8-0 type. It was the first time this wheel arrangement had been used in Britain and the G.W.R. engine was in many ways well ahead of its time. Production started in 1905 and eventually the 28XX class numbered 84 locomotives. Collett introduced a modernised version in 1938 and the combined class totalled 165 engines. Only the arrival of the B.R. 9F 2-10-0s displaced the 28XXs from their heavy goods supremacy, but there was work for them until the end of Western Region steam in 1965. Sixteen examples remain today in preservation.

L.M.S. 8F

2-8-0

Only 126 Stanier 8Fs had been constructed by the outbreak of World War II, but this modest total was soon transformed by the adoption of the class by the War Department as its chosen heavy freight engine for use at home and overseas. 51 were built by L.M.S. workshops and a further 208 by Beyer Peacock and North British for shipping abroad to assist the war effort. The majority were converted to oil firing and worked throughout the Middle East, keeping open the vital supply route from the Persian Gulf to the Caspian Sea.

MIXED TRAFFIC

Mixed traffic engine classes were a manifestation of the twentieth century and were brought about by two factors. Firstly, freight trains had increased in speed and were approaching the speed of some passenger trains. Secondly, the trend to rationalise within motive power fleets produced pressure for engines suitable for a wide range of duties. Such engines ultimately fulfilled most requirements on many of the world's railways, with the exception of the fastest passenger trains and the heaviest of freight.

Far from being versatile but anonymous 'maids of all work', however, many famous classes were actually mixed traffic engines equally at home hauling fast expresses and long distance freight. The Great Western 'Hall' and 'Manor' classes, the L.N.E.R. B1, the legendary 'Black 5' and even the West Country Pacifics, in both streamlined and re-built form, all fall into this category. All the B.R. Standard classes with the exception of the 9F, which was specifically designed for heavy mineral hauling, were mixed traffic engines. However, despite being sound and successful designs, many of them were destined to have their working lives cut short when the Railway Modernisation Plan of 1955 signalled the beginning of the end for steam in the UK.

L.M.S. 2MT
2-6-0

In 1946, George Ivatt produced for the L.M.S. its first truly modern small tender engine, capable of going just about anywhere thanks to its light axle loading. Up to date features of his Class 2 Moguls were rocking firegrates, self-emptying ashpans, self-cleaning smokeboxes and side-window cabs, all of which made life easier for the enginemen and shed staff. The enclosed tender cab and inset bunker made tender-first working more comfortable – inevitably the locomotives spent much of their time running in reverse on secondary lines without turntables.

L.M.S. 'BLACK 5'
4-6-0

Prompted by the success of the G.W.R. 'Hall' class 4-6-0s, William Stanier gave the design of a similar general purpose locomotive top priority on joining the L.M.S. from Swindon in 1932. It was just the type of standard locomotive that the railway needed to replace a mixed bag of ageing pre-grouping classes. So great was the need that the first orders were placed straight off the drawing board, with Crewe works and Vulcan Foundry sharing the work. The size and weight of the Class 5 gave it virtually unrestricted access to the entire L.M.S. system. It could be used on almost any duty from dealing with loose-coupled goods trains to express passenger services.

L.M.S. 2MT

2-6-0

By the end of 1953, 128 of the Ivatt Class 2 Moguls had entered service, with just over half the class constructed at Crewe. Operation of the little 2-6-0s was not confined to L.M.S. territory, however. A Darlington-built batch was allocated to the Eastern and North-Eastern Regions, whilst the last 25 were built at Swindon for use on the Western Region. Defiantly, these were turned out in lined green passenger livery rather than the prescribed mixed traffic black. They have proved understandably popular with preservationists, with seven of the class being saved to continue performing the type of duties they were built for.

S.R. 'WEST COUNTRY'

4-6-2

Essentially a scaled-down version of Bulleid's 'Merchant Navy' class of 1941, the first of his 'Light Pacifics' emerged from Brighton works in May 1945. The class was rapidly multiplied until no fewer than 110 were in service, most being named after locations in the west of England, but 44 locomotives were named after aircraft, airfields, RAF squadrons and personalities associated with the Battle of Britain. The 'Light Pacifics' shared many of the design features of the bigger 'Merchant Navies' but the principal differences were aimed at saving weight to allow them to operate almost anywhere on the southern system.

B1 'MAYFLOWER' SILHOUETTE

4-6-0

One of the two preserved L.N.E.R. Thompson B1 4-6-0s, No. 1306 'Mayflower', embodies the romance of the steam railway as it is silhouetted against the sunset at the head of a late afternoon train on the Great Central Railway. For many years whilst the former G.C.R. main line was under B.R. Eastern Region control, the B1s were regularly seen on all classes of train, heading north from London Marylebone bound for Leicester, Nottingham and Sheffield.

B.R. STANDARD 4MT

2-6-4T

Although designed at Brighton works, the handsome B.R. Standard Class 4MT tanks owed their pedigree to the Stanier and Fairburn tanks of the L.M.S. 155 examples were built, mostly at Brighton, and their brisk acceleration and lively turn of speed made them ideal for hauling tightly-timed commuter services, as they proved on the London, Tilbury and Southend line and on the Glasgow suburbans. Their versatility made them popular engines with the crews and no fewer than eight have survived in preservation.

G.W.R. 'MODIFIED HALL' NO. 6960

4-6-0

When F. W. Hawksworth succeeded Charles Collett at Swindon in 1941, his first design was an update of the 'Hall' class 4-6-0, marking the most significant change in G.W.R. practice since the Churchward era. The 'Modified Halls' of 1944 featured an altogether stronger front end with plate frames used throughout, a new plate-frame bogie and cylinders cast separately from the smokebox saddle. The boiler, too, benefited from a higher degree of superheat. In traffic, the engines were markedly superior to their forebears and 14 soldiered on to the end of Western Region steam in 1965. Seven of them have been preserved.

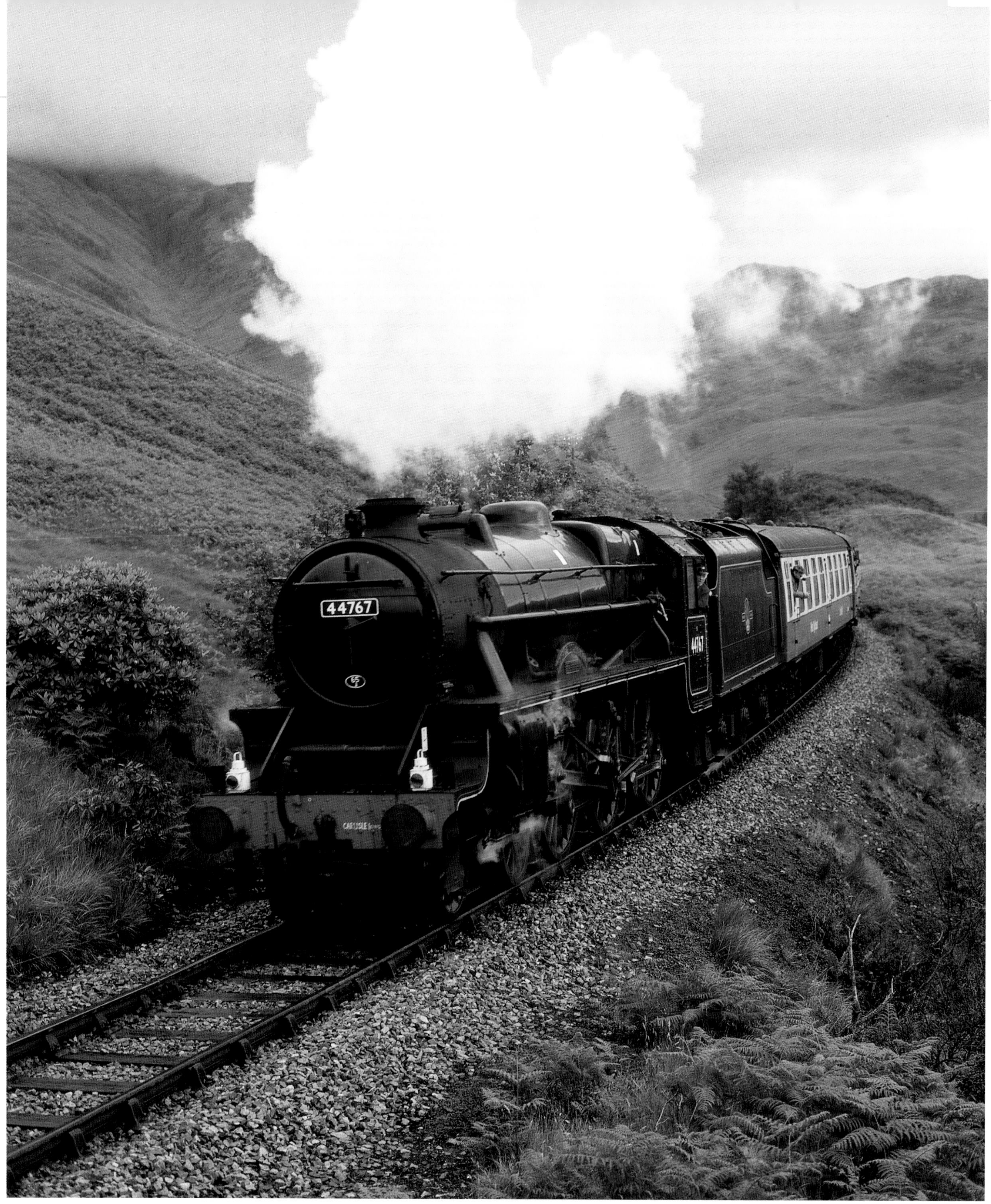
44767

L.M.S. 'BLACK 5'

4-6-0

Stanier's immediate successor, Charles Fairburn, continued to produce the 'Black 5' largely unaltered, but his replacement, George Ivatt, had other ideas. Ivatt brought out no less than eleven experimental versions of the class. The main variation occurred with Nos. 44738–57, which had Caprotti valve gear instead of the usual Walschaerts, whilst the now-preserved No. 44767 was equipped with Stephenson's outside link motion. Additionally, some engines were fitted with double blastpipes and chimneys, one received a steel firebox and others were used to assess the value of Timken and Skefco roller bearings.

L.N.E.R. B1 AND V2

4-6-0 and 2-6-2

The two principal L.N.E.R. mixed traffic classes were the Thompson B1 4-6-0 and the Gresley V2 2-6-2, examples of both types seen here in all too typical latter-day unkempt condition. The V2 must surely rank as one of Gresley's finest achievements. Essentially, it was a mixed traffic derivative of his magnificent three-cylinder P2 class Mikados, fitted with a shortened version of the A3 Pacific boiler. Thompson, working under wartime conditions, took the view that a two-cylinder machine with accessible motion parts was a more practical proposition and produced the B1 as an amalgam of standard L.N.E.R. components already in production.

G.W.R. 'MODIFIED HALL'
NO. 6990

As a brand new locomotive, No. 6990 'Witherslack Hall' took part in the 1948 locomotive exchange trials, working over the former Great Central main line on the Eastern Region. Despite the usefulness of such a versatile mixed traffic class, not a single example was selected for the National Collection so it was left to amateur enthusiasts to save what they could. No. 6990 was withdrawn from Bristol Barrow Road shed in 1965 and languished in Barry scrapyard for ten years before, appropriately enough, being restored to working order on the Great Central Railway.

FAIRBURN 42095 WITH
IVATT 2MT IN
BACKGROUND

2-6-4T

In a shed scene redolent of the last days of steam on British Railways, the motive power allocation is dominated by post-war L.M.S. designs. No. 42095 is one of the 277 Fairburn 4MT 2-6-4 tanks built in 1945 as a shorter-wheelbase development of Stanier's pre-war design. No. 46514 is one of the 25 Swindon-built Ivatt 2MT 2-6-0s whose modern labour-saving features and 'go anywhere' usefulness endeared them to crews and shed staff alike. An 8F and a 'Black 5' complete the scene.

L.N.E.R. K1

2-6-0

The 1945 rebuilding of Gresley's three-cylinder Mogul 'MacCailin Mor' with two cylinders was overseen by Arthur Peppercorn. When he succeeded Edward Thompson, he made the engine the prototype for this useful and versatile mixed traffic class. Although an L.N.E.R. design, they were all delivered after Nationalisation as B.R. 62001–70. They worked extensively over the North Eastern Region and on the West Highland line in Scotland, but dieselisation cut short their working lives and only one engine, No. 62005, survives in preservation.

L.M.S. 'BLACK 5'

4-6-0

The free-steaming qualities of the Class 5's boiler, combined with Stanier's careful attention to the valve events, comfortably allowed speeds of up to 90 mph. Besides the 75 engines originally ordered, the L.M.S. was responsible for the largest single locomotive building contract placed by a British railway company, when a further 227 engines were ordered from Armstrong Whitworth on Tyneside. By the end of 1938, there were 472 Class 5s at work. Construction resumed in 1943, and thereafter the workshops at Crewe, Derby and Horwich turned out batches every year until 1951, until no fewer than 842 engines were in traffic.

L.M.S. HUGHES 'CRAB'

2-6-0

George Hughes and his team at Horwich works produced the design for these celebrated mixed traffic Moguls and much of the locomotive was pure Lancashire & Yorkshire in concept and appearance. By the time the engines were in production in 1926, Hughes had retired and been succeeded by Henry Fowler from the Midland Railway. Fowler substituted many Midland fittings, including standard Derby tenders that were considerably narrower than the locomotives themselves. Nonetheless, the 'Horwich Moguls' were hard-working and efficient machines with 245 examples in traffic by 1932.

G.W.R. 'HALL'

4-6-0

The concept of a mixed traffic locomotive that was equally at home on freight or passenger trains was a novel one in the 1920s. When Charles Collett succeeded Churchward at Swindon in 1922, the latter's excellent but modestly sized 43XX class Moguls were finding traffic demands increasingly onerous. Collett's solution was to rebuild a 'Saint' class 4-6-0 with 6 ft (1.9 m) driving wheels, realigning the cylinders and fitting a side window cab. The rebuilt 'Saint Martin' emerged from Swindon in 1924 and became the prototype for the G.W.R.'s largest and most versatile mixed traffic class. In an interesting reversal of their genesis, the Great Western Society at Didcot is rebuilding No. 4942 'Maindy Hall' back into a 'Saint'.

L.N.E.R. B1

4-6-0

These were Edward Thompson's first new design for the L.N.E.R. and unquestionably his most successful. Produced under wartime conditions, the B1 was a two-cylinder locomotive sensibly incorporating many existing patterns and components. The prototype appeared in 1942, but it was only after the war that the class was expanded to 410 engines, mostly constructed by outside builders, with many being delivered after Nationalisation. Their wide route availability allowed distribution right across L.N.E.R. territory, working all classes of traffic from express passenger to parcels and freight.

S.R. 'U'

2-6-0

In August 1927, the disastrous Sevenoaks derailment of one of Richard Maunsell's 'K' class express 2-6-4Ts caused 20 planned additional locomotives to be built instead as 2-6-0 tender engines. Simultaneously, the 20 'K' class tanks were rebuilt as Moguls and incorporated into the new 'U' class. Eventually numbering 50 engines, the 'U' class, with their 6 ft (1.9 m) driving wheels, were employed throughout the Southern system. They were considered by enginemen to be the best of Maunsell's Moguls for passenger work and were noted for their exploits west of Exeter and on the Reading–Redhill line.

7819

G.W.R. 'MANOR'

4-6-0

Introduced in 1938, the 'Manors' were the smallest and lightest of the Great Western 4-6-0s, permitted to run over routes barred to their larger sisters. Although equipped with a new design of boiler, the wheels, motion and tenders for the locomotives were recovered from scrapped Churchward 43XX class Moguls. Thirty engines entered service, the last ten being built after Nationalisation. They were principally associated with services in mid-Wales, with their most prestigious working the 'Cambrian Coast Express' which they hauled from Shrewsbury to Aberystwyth.

G.W.R. 2251

0-6-0

When G. J. Churchward set out his plans for his standard family of locomotives for the G.W.R. in the early years of the 20th century, he had no thoughts of providing replacements for 2301 class 'Dean Goods' 0-6-0s of 1883, which were thus to soldier on in unspectacular fashion on pick-up goods and local passenger trains for the next three decades. By 1930, they were beginning to show their age and Collett drew up a modern version incorporating a superheated taper boiler. This was the 2251 class, and its 120 members gradually assumed the duties of their predecessors.

BULLEID REBUILT 'LIGHT PACIFIC'

By 1957, the level of maintenance demanded by such problematic mechanisms as chain-driven valve gear could not be justified, and a scheme was drawn up to rebuild 60 of the Bulleid 'Light Pacifics' along the same lines as the 'Merchant Navies'. The fundamental changes were the substitution of Walschaerts valve gear and the removal of the air-smoothed casing. Thus rejuvenated, the rebuilt engines put in fine performances right up to the last day of Southern steam in July 1967. Remarkably, no fewer than 20 of the type have passed into preservation, nine of them in unrebuilt condition.

G.W.R. 2251

0-6-0

The G.W.R. never used 0-6-0 tender engines to the same extent as other railways, relying on their 2-6-0s for most mixed traffic, intermediate work. The 2251 class relieved the 'Dean Goods' locomotives of their duties on unrestricted routes so that these older, smaller engines could be concentrated on the Cambrian section. As well as handling goods traffic, the Collett engines took their turn with passenger work over the longer cross-country routes, such as the Didcot, Newbury & Southampton and Somerset & Dorset routes. No. 3205 was retired from Templecombe (S. & D.) shed in 1965 and preserved in working order.

S.R. BULLEID 'LIGHT PACIFIC'

When new, Bulleid's Pacifics bristled with novel features. The 'air-smoothed' casing was intended to be cleaned by passing through the carriage washing plant rather than being an attempt at streamlining. The 'boxpok' wheel centres saved over a third of the weight of conventional wheels. The magnificent 280 lb (126 kg) boiler contained an all-welded steel firebox fitted with thermic syphons, to improve water circulation. There was a Lemaitre multiple-jet blastpipe, rocking firegrate, electric lighting and of course the innovative chain-driven valve gear. To give it even more visual impact, the locomotive was finished in bright malachite green paintwork with broad yellow stripes.

S.R. BULLEID 'LIGHT PACIFIC'

During the locomotive exchange trials which took place soon after Nationalisation, the Bulleid 'Light Pacifics' put up performances equal or superior to any of their larger rivals from other lines. Developing nearly 2,000 horsepower at the drawbar, they showed an ability to make up time hauling heavy trains over adverse gradients, though at the expense of heavy coal and oil consumption. On their home territory, the 'Light Pacifics' were used on almost every Southern passenger working from the 'Golden Arrow' down to two- and three-coach local trains in Cornwall.

L.M.S. 'BLACK 5'

4-6-0

Stanier Black 5s could be found everywhere on the former L.M.S. system from Bournemouth on the Somerset & Dorset line to Wick and Thurso in Scotland. North of Perth on the Highland lines, Black 5s were the largest and heaviest engines permitted, and here they handled most trains of significance from the 550-tonne 'Royal Highlander' downwards. After Nationalisation their spheres of activity were extended to the West Highland line, and a few were called on to deputise for Southern Bulleid Pacifics when these were under investigation for technical problems in the 1950s.

L.M.S. 'BLACK 5'

4-6-0

As well as exhibiting variations in valve gear and exhaust arrangements, the postwar L.M.S. 'Black 5s' incorporated devices that were to become obligatory on the B.R. Standard designs: self-cleaning smokeboxes, rocking grates and self-emptying ashpans. And of course, the 'Black 5' itself became the basis for Robert Riddles' B.R. 5MT 4-6-0, totalling another 172 locomotives, which are the obvious descendants of the L.M.S. engines.

BRANCH LINE
&
SUBURBAN TRAINS

Whilst the main lines provide fast, efficient links between major towns and cities, travel within conurbations or in rural areas is provided by a network of secondary and branch lines. The need for these was brought about by the need to get people to and from their homes and places of work after the Industrial Revolution. Until the advent of motor transport, the branch line was the only way for the population of rural areas to take excursions beyond the confines of their village, sometimes for the first time, and this further accelerated the drift from the country to the town.

Such suburban services were best worked by tank engines, as these were able to run easily in either direction and had small wheels in order to start rapidly after their frequent station stops. The tank engines were supplemented by cross-country engines that served the secondary interconnecting lines that joined up the main arteries, as well as the branch lines that were built at around the same time. These engines were often similar to those used for suburban work, although, as new classes came into service, downgraded main line engines often found a new lease of life running on secondary and branch lines.

C.R. NO. 55195 AT KILLIN
0-4-4T

The engineering legacy of Dugald Drummond endured on the Caledonian Railway long after his departure. Drummond himself was much influenced by his mentor, William Stroudley, and it is easy to see both men's design hallmarks of rounded tank tops, leading splasher sandboxes and elegant but narrow cab in the family of 0-4-4 tanks produced by his successors at St Rollox works. John Lambie's '19' class of 1895 was quickly followed by the more numerous but virtually identical McIntosh '439' class of 1900. William Pickersgill added his own version of the latter class and there was even a batch of ten built by the L.M.S. in 1925.

L.B. & S.C.R. STROUDLEY 'TERRIER'

Introduced in 1872, William Stroudley's A1 class 'Terriers' gained their reputation on the snappily-timed East London line suburban trains. Thirty years on, nearly half the class of fifty engines found eager second-hand buyers, such as the Newhaven Harbour Co., the Isle of Wight Railways and three of Colonel Stephens' legendary light railways. They were still working on the Isle of Wight into the British Railways era, and were also the mainstays of the Hayling Island branch in Hampshire. No fewer than ten have found their way into preservation.

H. & M. '7'
0-4-4T

Most of the major railway companies running suburban services into the London terminals adopted the 0-4-4T as it gave the opportunity to fit a reasonable-sized boiler on a bogie chassis, giving good riding qualities when running in reverse. For the S.E. & C.R. commuter trains into Charing Cross, Harry Wainwright provided his pretty H class, whilst over at Waterloo, Dugald Drummond's somewhat larger M7s were in charge. Suburban electrification displaced both types onto rural and secondary duties and over a third of each class were fitted for push-pull working. Nearly all were retained as reliable branch line engines by British Railways, resulting in examples of both classes surviving in active preservation.

B.R. STANDARD 4MT

4-6-0

As with the majority of the B.R. Standard designs, the 4MT 4-6-0 drew heavily on postwar L.M.S. practice. 80 engines were built at Swindon between 1951 and 1957 and shared between the London Midland, Western and Southern Regions, the latter receiving locomotives paired with high-sided 4725-gallon tenders, as none of the Southern routes had water troughs. The class was widely used on secondary and cross-country routes. Their most celebrated exploits came on the former Cambrian Railways main line from Shrewsbury to Aberystwyth and Pwllheli, where they worked alongside and matched the performance of the G.W.R. 'Manors'.

NORTH LONDON RAILWAY '75'

0-6-0T

J. C. Park introduced his '75' class short wheelbase 0-6-0Ts in 1879 to negotiate the tightly curved sidings in London's Dockland. They were remarkably powerful machines and continued to work at Poplar docks until the mid-1950s. However, back in 1931, the L.M.S. had sent two to work on the Cromford & High Peak line in Derbyshire, where their short wheelbase and abundant power made them ideally suited to the fearsome C. & H.P. gradients and further engines were relocated from London. In 1960 the last survivor, No. 58850, was saved for preservation on the Bluebell Railway.

L.S.W.R. O2

0-4-4T

William Adams' medium-sized 'O2' suburban tanks were introduced in 1889, but after only a decade were displaced from many of their duties by Drummond's much larger M7 class. However, their modest size and lively acceleration made them ideal candidates to revitalise the Isle of Wight services and 21 were shipped across by the Southern Railway. Fitted with Westinghouse brakes and extended bunkers and carrying Island names, the O2s lasted in service until the end of Isle of Wight steam in 1966. No. W24 'Calbourne' was saved for preservation on the Isle of Wight Steam Railway.

G.W.R. 14XX

0-4-2T

The G.W.R. adopted the practice of replacing older engines with new ones of the same basic design and in this instance, old '517' class 0-4-2Ts built between 1868 and 1897 were replaced in service by 95 new engines constructed between 1932 and 1936. They took over from their predecessors on the numerous Great Western branch lines and stopping train services, and proved quick and efficient in operation. The advent of the diesel railcar and the closure of many branch lines rendered many of them redundant and withdrawals began in 1956.

G.W.R. 45XX

2-6-2T

In many ways the ideal branch line locomotive, Churchward's 'Small Prairie' tanks clearly inspired later L.M.S. and B.R. standard designs. The 45XX class appeared from Swindon in 1906 and 55 examples were built. Churchward's successor, Charles Collett, enlarged the design to incorporate bigger water capacity and 100 examples of this 4575 class were delivered between 1926 and 1929. Both classes served the G.W.R. and its successors well on the picturesque West Country branch lines and withdrawals did not begin until 1950. The last survivors worked until 1964, allowing three of the 45XX class and no fewer than 11 of the 4575s to be preserved.

W. & L.L.R.

0-6-0T

These compact and sturdy little engines were built by Beyer Peacock for the opening of the 2'6" gauge Welshpool & Llanfair Light Railway in Wales are still at work on the line today. 'The Earl' and 'The Countess', named in honour of the Earl and Countess of Powis, handled all the traffic on the steeply-graded line from its opening in 1903 to closure in 1956. Although somewhat 'Great Westernised' in appearance, they retain many of their classic Gorton features. When the line was closed by British Railways, both locomotives were taken to Oswestry works, returning to Llanfair in triumph when the railway reopened in 1963.

G.W.R. 57XX
0-6-0PT

Equally at home hauling branch line passenger trains, in later years a handful of the numerous 57XX panniers ventured away from the Western Region, undertaking banking work on the Folkestone Harbour incline and pilot duties at Waterloo. Some surplus engines were sold to the National Coal Board and in 1956 London Transport began acquiring them to replace former Metropolitan Railway locomotives on shunting work and engineers' trains. A total of 14 pannier tanks saw L.T. service and three of these remained at work until 1971. This trio now numbers among the 16 survivors that continue to prove their worth in preservation.

C.R.
0-4-4T

The Caledonian 0-4-4Ts of Drummond and his successors became a byword for simplicity, rugged construction and reliability and were very long-lived. Examples of all four classes were still active well after Nationalisation and when the last McIntosh '439' class survivor, B.R. No. 55189, was withdrawn, it was saved by the Scottish Railway Preservation Society. The locomotive has been restored in full Caledonian blue livery as No. 419 and operates on the Bo'ness & Kinneil Railway.

ISLE OF MAN BEYER PEACOCK

2-4-0T

The design of these charming little engines was derived from very similar 3'6" gauge machines Beyer Peacock supplied to the Norwegian State Railway in 1871. The Manx engines were developed in four distinct stages over a period of half a century, each subsequent batch being of larger capacity to cope with the ever-increasing volume of traffic on the island's railways. An identical locomotive supplied to the Manx Northern Railway in 1880 was later acquired by the I.M.R. as their No. 14 'Thornhill', whilst two others of the same design were built for the Ballymena & Larne Railway in Ireland.

L.M.S. 2MT

2-6-2T

On the Southern Region, Ivatt's handsome little Class 2 2-6-2Ts were the most modern passenger tanks available and displaced elderly pre-Grouping engines, often being rostered for duties intended for more powerful locomotives. It was the S.R.'s engines which lasted in service the longest (until 1967) and four of these have survived in preservation. Two have been restored to working order: No. 41241 on the Keighley & Worth Valley Railway and No. 41312 on the Mid-Hants Railway.

57XX PANNIER TANKS AT PENTIR RHIW

The ubiquitous 57XX Pannier tanks settled in well in south Wales and in their later years monopolised services over the former Brecon & Merthyr route with its formidable climb of eight miles at 1 in 40 from Talybont-on-Usk to Torpantau. A crossing loop and platform with minimal facilities was provided halfway up the ascent, adjoining the signal box at Pentir Rhiw, where 9776 pauses with a brakevan to allow 3661 to pass on a Newport–Brecon passenger train.

FESTINIOG RAILWAY DOUBLE-FAIRLIE

The rapid growth of slate traffic on the Festiniog Railway soon called for something stronger than its small George England 0-4-0Ts of 1863. The answer was a 'double engine', a design patented by Robert Fairlie. In this, a twin boiler unit sharing a central firebox was mounted on the mainframe supported on two power bogies. The driver and fireman occupied a central cab, with one man on either side of the firebox. Four engines were built between 1869 and 1885, the last pair being constructed at the company's Boston Lodge works.

WAINWRIGHT H ON BLUEBELL

0-4-4

Harry Wainwright's H class 0-4-4 tanks were particularly elegant in appearance, particularly when attired in full South Eastern & Chatham Railway livery. When new, they were allocated to London suburban work, where they displaced older S.E.R. and L.C.D.R. classes of 0-4-4T. As class numbers multiplied, they could be seen on Tonbridge–London semi-fasts via Redhill and on stopping trains on the Hastings line. In later years, they were much associated with branch line work on the Eastern and Brighton sections where they quickly became firm favourites with their crews.

L.S.W.R. ADAMS RADIAL TANKS

4-4-2T

William Adams advocated using a leading bogie in his locomotives and his first design was a 4-4-0 suburban tank, soon extended over a radial trailing axle to become a 4-4-2T. The 59 engines of his '415' class of 1882 successfully developed this theme, but their time hauling London commuters was comparatively brief, being supplanted by later. Withdrawals began in 1916 and all had gone by the mid-1920s except two retained for working the tortuous Lyme Regis branch in Dorset. A third engine was bought back from Col. Stephens' East Kent Railway, and the trio worked the branch until 1961. Ex-E.K.R. No. 488 was saved for preservation by the Bluebell Railway.

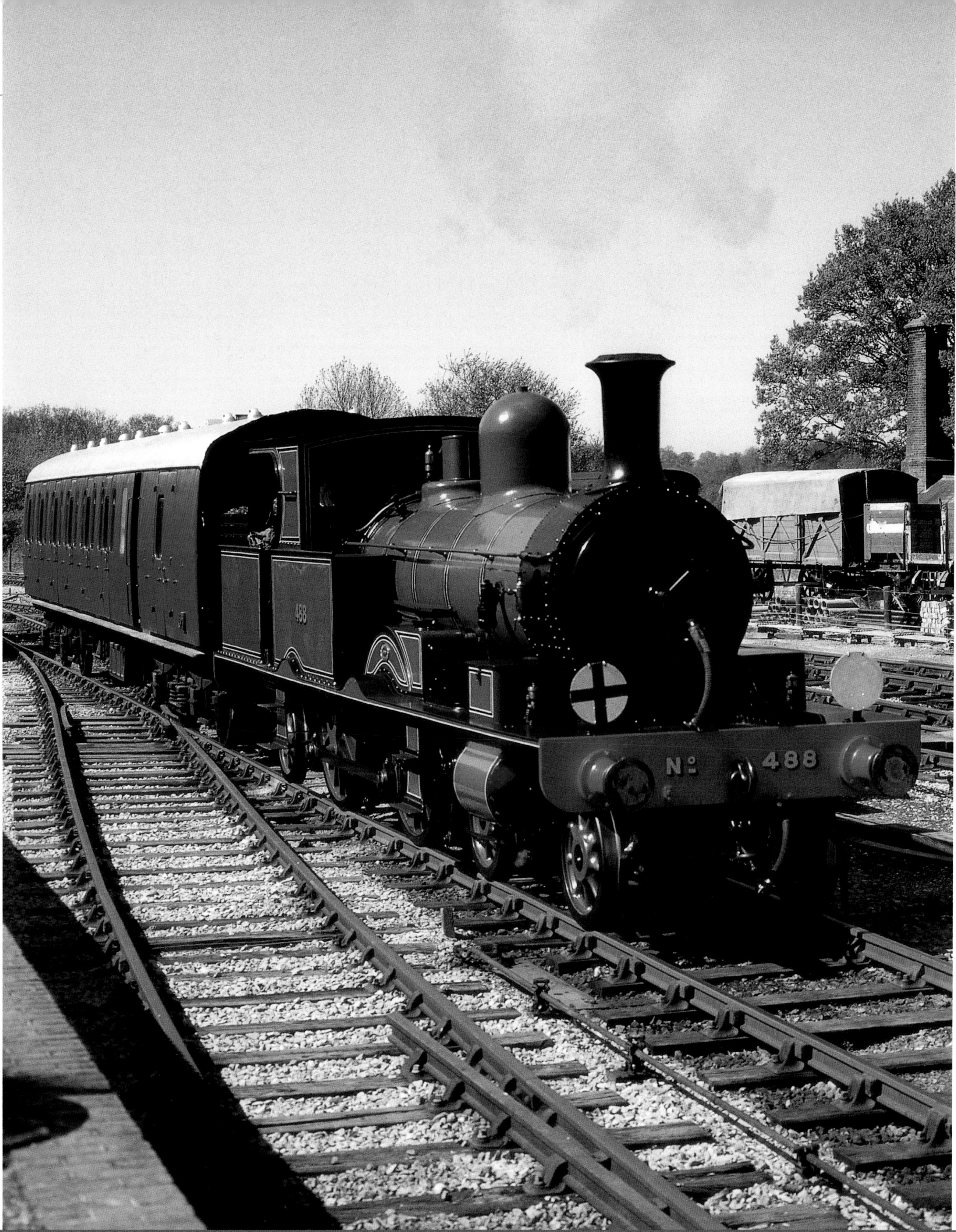
488
No 488

L.N.E.R. GRESLEY N2

0-6-2T

The Gresley N2 tanks were synonymous with London's King's Cross suburban services. Constricted tunnels between King's Cross and Moorgate imposed height and length restrictions on the design, resulting in a compact, powerful locomotive with large, superheated boiler, capable of impressive acceleration with the trains of high-capacity articulated coaches. 107 were built between 1920 and 1929, and over a decade after Nationalisation were still in charge of King's Cross suburban traffic. The arrival of diesel multiple-unit trains saw their rapid demise, however, and by 1962 the last had gone for scrap. No. 69523 has survived to represent the class in preservation.

G.W.R. 61XX

2-6-2T

There were several G.W.R. classes of large 2-6-2T built for suburban passenger work, the 61XX class of 1931 being the final development and most powerful of its type. For many years the whole class of 70 engines worked entirely in the London division, the vast majority from Southall, Slough and Old Oak Common sheds. Introduced to replace ageing 4-4-2 and 2-4-0 tanks, the 61XX class proved highly successful and several of the class survived until the last day of steam traction on the Western Region.

L.N.W.R. 'COAL TANK'

Under F. W. Webb, Crewe works became synonymous with ruthless cost control, standardisation and mass production of a family of austere and dignified locomotives. His 'Coal Tanks' of 1881 were strong and workmanlike and despite their name, were widely used on passenger as well as goods work. 300 examples were built over a period of 17 years and their capacity for hard work left over 60 in traffic at Nationalisation, distributed across the former L.N.W.R. system between Lancashire and south Wales. The last 'Coal Tank' retired as B.R. No. 58926 in 1958 and was saved for posterity.

L.M.S. 2MT

2-6-2T

In the final years of the L.M.S., George Ivatt designed his Class 2 tank – arguably Britain's best branch-line locomotive. Undoubtedly inspired by Churchward's G.W.R. 45XX Prairie tank of 1906, they incorporated many technical advances made during the intervening 40 years. Only the first ten locomotives wore L.M.S. livery, the remaining 120 being built after Nationalisation. In service their usefulness was recognised far and wide – as well as being spread throughout former L.M.S. territory, the Southern Region's sizeable allocation could be found everywhere between Kent and Cornwall.

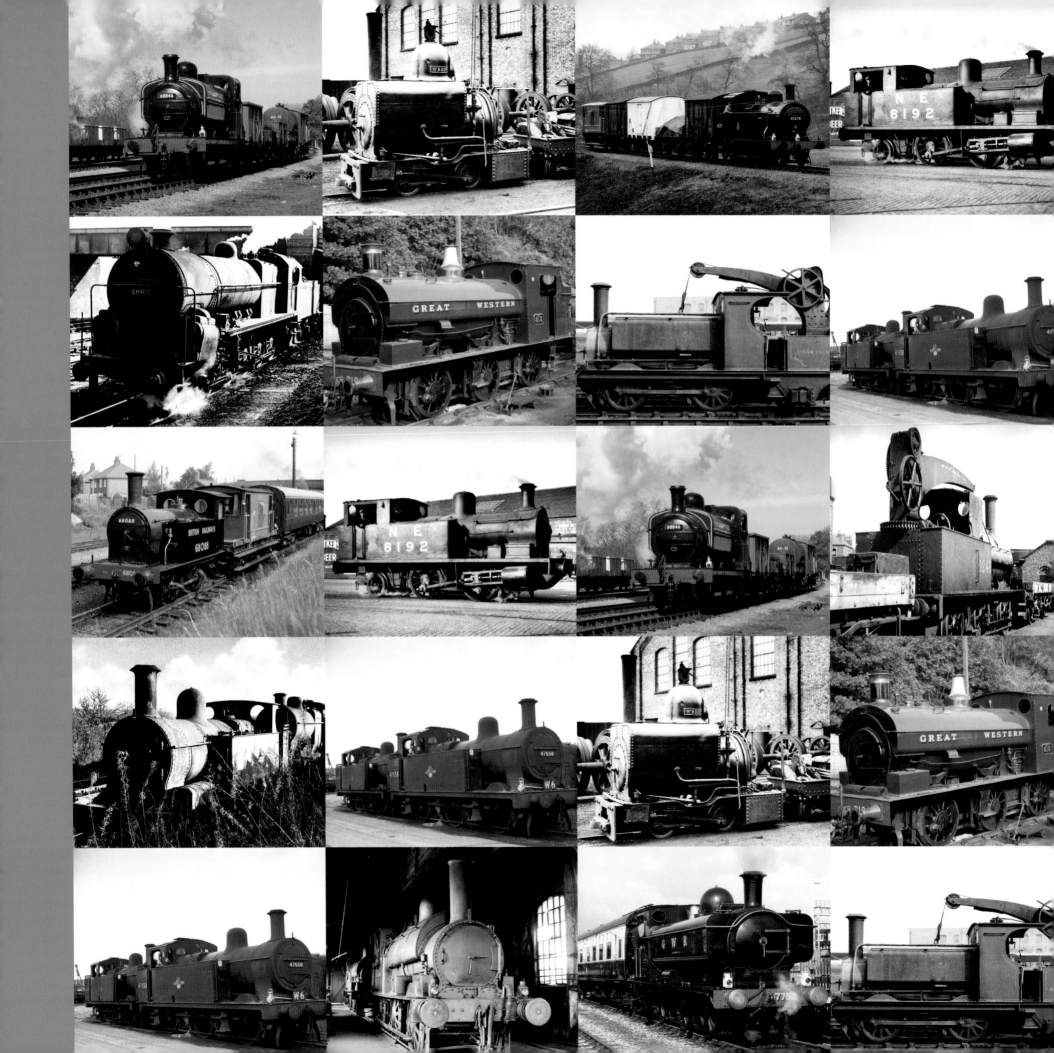

SHUNTERS

Railway rolling stock is heavy and rugged and capable of withstanding rigorous use in the most arduous conditions. It was this weight that posed problems when stock needed to be assembled into a train or moved around from one part of the stock yard to another, and as the stock was often in diverse places within the yard, the need for specialised shunting engines became apparent.

These were designed for maximum adhesion and easy manoeuvrability. They were invariably tank engines that were capable of moving carriages and wagons easily around the marshalling yards and large sidings which were established once railway networks had developed, and an interchange of movements became necessary. They were equally capable of providing a hefty shove to move rakes of stock many times their own weight, yet in the hands of an experienced driver, give the most deft and delicate final touch to close up the coupling. It was also common practice to utilise down-graded and out-winded freight engines for shunting duties, and, as the age of steam came to a close, many such engines gravitated into shunting yards.

L.N.W.R. RAMSBOTTOM 'SPECIAL TANKS'

0-6-0ST

This long-lived class of 0-6-0STs were built at Crewe in considerable numbers from 1870 onwards and were the standard shunting engine for many years throughout the L.N.W.R. Indeed, five of them continued in departmental service until after Nationalisation, with the last survivors shunting at Wolverton Carriage Works until 1959. Six examples were built with slightly larger driving wheels to 5'3" gauge between 1873 and 1898 for use on the L.N.W.R.'s Irish offshoot, the Dundalk, Newry & Greenore Railway. These hauled all the traffic on the line until 1933, and the last survivors remained in action until 1952. To the end they retained their old L.N.W.R. livery and characteristics.

MIDLAND RAILWAY LICKEY BANKER

0-10-0

In complete contrast to its otherwise 'small engine' policy, in 1919 the Midland Railway produced by far its largest locomotive. No. 2290 (nicknamed 'Big Bertha') was a four-cylinder 0-10-0 engine built specially for banking trains up the Lickey incline with its three miles of continuous 1 in 37 ascent, and which had hitherto seen nothing larger than 0-6-0Ts on this duty. It remained the sole example of its type, with a spare boiler kept in readiness at Derby to keep its works visits as short as possible. After 36 years of heavy pounding up the bank, it was withdrawn from service in 1956.

G.W.R. (PORT TALBOT) NO. 813

0-6-0ST

A locomotive which owes its continued existence to its long and adventurous working life is 0-6-0ST No. 813 of the former Port Talbot Railway. Delivered from Hudswell Clarkes of Leeds in 1901, it became G.W.R. property in 1923 and during the course of overhauls at Swindon, acquired various standard G.W.R. fittings. It is thus a prime example of the 'Swindonised' appearance of absorbed locomotives following the grouping. In 1934, however, it was sold out of service to Backworth Colliery in Northumberland where it put in another 34 years' work before being bought for preservation.

NORTH LONDON RAILWAY CRANE TANK

0-4-2

This engine started life in 1858 as a small 0-4-0ST built by Sharp Stewart & Co. for working between Hammersmith and Acton. It was taken over by the N.L.R. shortly afterwards and rebuilt in 1872 with an additional trailing axle supporting a crane, and in this form it spent the next eighty years of its life as works shunter at Bow. It became the oldest engine inherited by British Railways at Nationalisation and there were hopes that it would achieve its working centenary. But alas, the little crane tank was withdrawn in 1951 and sent to Derby where it remained for several months before being scrapped.

G.N.R. J52

0-6-0ST

For almost a century, the G.N.R. and its successors relied on six-coupled saddletanks for shunting and local goods work. The final development of the type came in 1897 when Henry Ivatt introduced his J13 class, an enlarged version of earlier Stirling engines. Further examples came from outside builders until 1909, when the class numbered 85 engines. Apart from shunting the goods yards in London and alongside the East Coast main line, they were employed on transfer freights across the capital; duties that were inevitably taken over by diesel shunters and large numbers were retired in the late 1950s. No. 1247 was bought for preservation by Captain Bill Smith in 1959.

TWO 'JINTIES' AT CREWE

Since 1874 the Midland Railway had standardised on six-coupled side tanks for shunting work. Samuel Johnson produced an enlarged version in 1899 and these were later rebuilt with Belpaire fireboxes and improved cabs. These rebuilds were adopted as the pattern for the L.M.S. 3F tank of 1924. A total of 422 engines were built over the next six years and the duties they undertook – shunting, trip freights, banking, station pilot work, local passenger – were the bread and butter work of the railway. They were distributed widely across the L.M.S. system and two were later deputed to become the Crewe works shunters.

G.N. OF S.R. Z5

0-4-2T

These two engines were supplied by Manning Wardle & Co. for the inauguration of locomotive haulage on the Aberdeen Harbour lines in 1915. They were neat little outside-cylindered side tanks, but on arrival were found to be two tonnes heavier than specified. Two slightly smaller versions (Class Z4) were ordered from the same makers, but the heavier engines were retained and all four spent their working lives in Aberdeen docks. Both classes retained their pre-grouping livery until 1939, thereafter becoming plain black under L.N.E.R. and B.R. ownership.

G.W.R. 57XX

0-6-0PT

Distinct from other main line railways, the Great Western preferred to equip its tank engines with pannier tanks slung either side of the boiler. Thanks to the wealth of small tank engines already owned by the G.W.R. when the first pannier tanks appeared in 1898, Churchward saw no need for large-scale construction. Many of the early locomotives were worn out by 1929, however, so Collett introduced the 57XX class as an enlarged and improved version of Churchward's engines. Swindon works and outside builders constructed a massive total of 863 locomotives over the next 17 years. They were equally at home on shunting work, local goods trains, handling empty coaching stock or on branch lines.

HORWICH WORKS 'WREN'

0-4-0ST

The Horwich works 18' gauge railway system first came into being when the works itself was opened in 1887. So successful was the system that it was considerably enlarged over the next three decades and at its peak, around the time of World War I, nearly 7 miles of track were in use. The next 30 years brought a protracted era of decline, however, during which the complement of eight diminutive steam locomotives had been reduced to one. By 1962, the sole survivor, the 1887 Beyer Peacock 0-4-0ST 'Wren', had became B.R.'s smallest steam locomotive and was preserved in the National Collection.

L.N.W.R. CRANE TANK NOS. 3247 & 3248

0-4-2

For moving heavy materials as well as performing general shunting duties around a locomotive works yard, a crane tank locomotive is an indispensable piece of railway equipment, so F. W. Webb designed a pair of 0-4-2 saddle tanks for duties at Crewe in 1892. These useful machines had their crane mounted at the rear of the coal bunker, but to permit them to travel out onto the running lines of the L.N.W.R., the crane jib could not be raised, but could of course slew through 360 degrees. They had long and useful lives, the last being withdrawn in 1946.

N.E.R. Y7

0-4-0T

Thomas Worsdell's diminutive H class tanks were built to negotiate the tightly-curved tracks at the N.E.R.'s seaports along the east coast. These sturdy four-coupled side tanks with domeless boilers and open-backed cabs proved ideal for dock shunting work. The first six engines emerged from Gateshead works in 1888, with further batches appearing in 1891 and 1897 and, surprisingly, a last batch of five in 1923. Half the class of 24 engines were sold into industrial service after 1929, working mainly at mines and quarries well into their old age. Two that became National Coal Board property have survived in active preservation.

L.M.S. 3F

0-6-0T

For almost 40 years, the Fowler 3F tanks performed a multitude of vital basic duties for the L.M.S. and British Railways. From the crew's point of view, they were comfortable engines with a free-steaming boiler and were a pleasure to drive. No. 47279, built in 1924, spent most of its working lifetime around Bedford and Wellingborough, though its most northerly posting was Workington. This engine is one of ten preserved representatives of the class and is based on the Keighley & Worth Valley Railway.

JOHNSON 1F

0-6-0T

The '1377' class was S.W. Johnson's first design after coming to the Midland Railway, and 40 were supplied by Neilsons and Vulcan Foundry in 1874–76. Many more followed from Derby, and still further batches from other builders until 1899, by which time the class totalled 185 engines. The majority were fitted with open-back 'half-cabs', by which name the class became known. Under a contract signed in 1866, the Midland Railway undertook to supply shunting locomotives to Staveley Ironworks in Derbyshire for 100 years. British Railways inherited that obligation and retained five of the 'Half-cabs' to perform the work. This allowed the opportunity for No. 41708 to be preserved.

Overseas Exports

Britain was railway builder to an empire and the world, as it exported its Industrial Revolution around the globe. In distant lands, vast manufactories were built to provide locomotives and rolling stock, along with the enormous infrastructure needed to develop railways in all kinds of terrain.

As a result, the British influence was all pervasive and led to British designs and standards being found not only throughout the empire, but also in countries under the British sphere of influence such as Sudan, Brazil and Argentina. Locomotives that were recognizably Gresley-based were also to be found on the railways of India. Until quite recently some of the oldest working locomotives in the world, all exported from famous British manufacturers such as Beyer Peacock, Vulcan Foundry, Hunslet and Beardmore, could be found working in such diverse locations as sugar mills, on port systems or in thermal power stations. The list of manufacturers worksplates to be seen on engines all around the world reads like a who's who of UK locomotive builders of the nineteenth and twentieth centuries.

Britain's conceiving, designing, building, exporting and operating of railways worldwide constitutes one of the greatest achievements of the Industrial Revolution and one of the proudest chapters in British history.

PAKISTAN RAILWAYS
SPS (1)
4-4-0

The Pakistan Railways SPS Class inside cylinder 4-4-0s were essentially typical Manchester locomotives, being very similar to the Manchester, Sheffield & Lincolnshire Railway's 4-4-0s designed a few years previously by Henry Pollitt. M.S.L.R.'s works were located in the Manchester suburb of Gorton, immediately opposite those of the private locomotive builder Beyer Peacock. The M.S.L.R.'s main line ran between the two works which were connected by an overbridge. It is therefore easy to see how Britain's classic homespun design influences were spread to far away countries around the world.

BEYER PEACOCK, BRAZIL
2-6-0

Fifty of these pretty 2-6-0s were built in 1899–1900 by Beyer Peacock for Brazil's metre gauge Leopoldina Railway. Long since disappeared from main line service, this wood burning example ended up working at the Usina Santa Maria sugarmill in Campos state and was almost certainly the last survivor of its type. Notice how the original Beyer Peacock chimney has been eaten away over some ninety years as a result of the engine's constant fiery endeavours.

15A, ARGENTINA

Argentina's 15A Class consisted of eight oil burning mixed traffic locomotives, built in 1939 for the 5' 6" gauge by the Vulcan Foundry in Lancashire. Their boilers, bogies and tenders were identical to the 12K Class Pacifics built the same year. Originally the 15As were fitted with smoke deflectors but these were later removed. Four examples were built with Caprotti valve gear but this too was later removed in favour of Walschaerts. The 15As were very successful on the Buenos Aires to Mar del Plata night trains and particularly on the legendary fruit hauls from the Rio Negro valley. All were named and some examples survived until the 1980s.

S160, GREECE

The latter day standard gauge steam roster of Greece was full of fascinating diversities combining classic 0-10-0 and 2-10-0 designs. These were derived from the drawing board of the legendary Karl Golsdorf, C.M.E. of the Austrian State Railway, British-built locomotives from World War II, and a stud of Major Marsh's S160 2-8-0s, built for the United States Army Transportation Corps. Built to the British loading gauge, upwards of 2,500 of these S160s were put into traffic from the American builders Baldwin, Alco and Lima. These engines operated throughout the war zone and following the conflict, some fifty, classified Theta Gamma, were incorporated into Greek Railway stock. Survivors remained at work until the 1970s.

BE, ARGENTINA
0-6-0ST

These BE Class 0-6-0STs were a typically British shunting engine for Argentina's 5' 6" gauge railways. They were first introduced from the North British Works in Glasgow in 1904 with subsequent examples being built by Kerr Stewart and Co., Stoke-on-Trent. The BEs had a delightful Scottish aura and appeared to be a larger version of the Caledonian Railway's celebrated 0-4-0 Pugs. This engine, seen on shed at Bahia Blanca, was the last survivor of the class.

MIKADO 310, SUDAN

Britain's most important legacy to Sudan was a vast and superbly run railway network. This extended from Wadi Halfa, close to the Egyptian border in the north, to Wau, an incredible 1,457 miles to the south. Following independence in 1956, the railway underwent gradual deterioration to the great detriment of the nation. The system possessed a superb stud of blue liveried, 3' 6" gauge locomotives which contrasted well with the golden tones of the surrounding desert. These 310 Class Mikados date back to 1952 and along with many of Sudan's locomotives came from the North British Works in Glasgow.

INDIAN RAILWAYS
SGC2/XC

Two classic Indian locomotive types for the sub-continent's 5' 6" gauge main lines are shown here. The inside cylinder 0-6-0 on the left was one of a type originally introduced by the B.E.S.A. standardisation programme of 1903 and was built by the Vulcan Foundry at Newton le Willows, Lancashire for the East Indian Railway in 1913. The handsome XC Class Pacific on the right, built in 1928, also by the Vulcan Foundry, was one of the famous 'X Series' standards of the 1920s. The XCs were the last large British express passenger engines left in world service and survived in Bengal until the 1980s. None have been preserved.

ISLE OF MAN
2-4-0T

One of the world's most delightful enclaves of steam traction is on the Isle of Man, with its 3' gauge Beyer Peacock 2-4-0Ts, dating back to 1873 when the railway opened. Of typical Beyer Peacock design, they were a smaller version of the company's standard gauge 4-4-0Ts built in 1864 for the Metropolitan Railway for use on the first suburban workings in London. The Isle of Man Steam Railway is one of the island's greatest tourist attractions and a journey in its vintage vehicles through the unspoiled landscape, hauled by these period 2-4-0s, is unforgettable.

NORTH BRITISH MOGUL, PARAGUAY

These delightful Edwardian Moguls, built in the Glasgow suburb of Springburn during the Edwardian period, have monopolised services over Paraguay's standard gauge main line for three quarters of a century. They work from Asuncion, the Paraguayan capital, to Encarnacion on the Argentinean border and having crossed the river Posadas by ferry, some coaches proceed via Argentinean Railways to Buenos Aires. In Paraguay, these Moguls are true mixed traffic engines handling both freight trains and passenger trains alike. In 1953 two more examples were built based on the original design by the Yorkshire Engine Company's Meadowhall Works in Sheffield.

'MERSEY', INDIA
0-4-0

This remarkable 0-4-0 tender engine, surviving at an Indian sugarmill, was for many years the oldest locomotive left in world service. She was built in 1873 by Sharp Stewart at their Great Bridgewater Street works in Manchester – fourteen years before the company moved to Glasgow – and when 'Mersey' was exported from Liverpool docks, Queen Victoria would rule the British Empire for another 28 years. 'Mersey' was originally built for the metre gauge Tirhut Railway, and in 1874 provided important famine relief by connecting Tirhut with Patna, a hundred miles away.

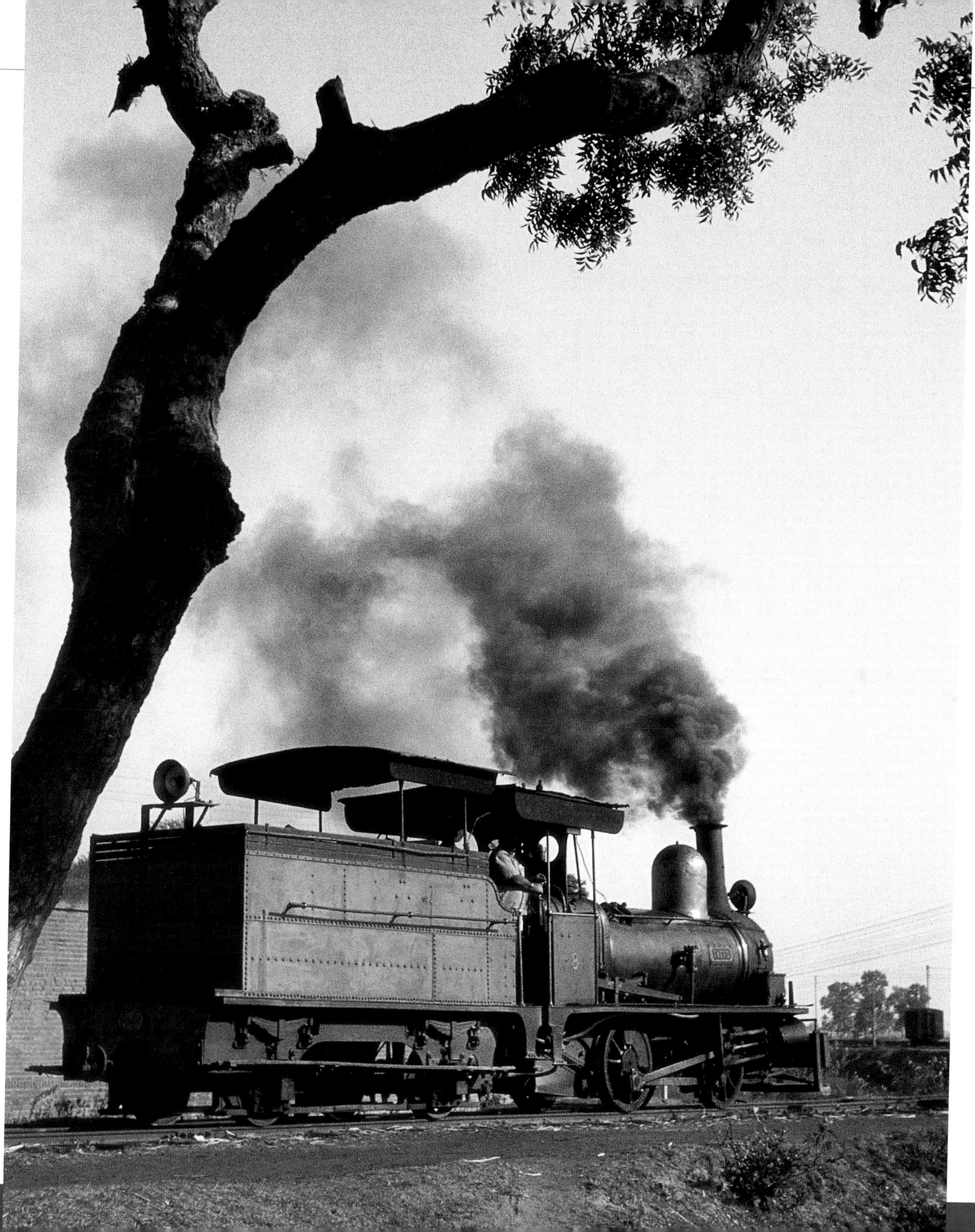

KENYA RAILWAY,
MOUNTAIN GARRATTS

These metre gauge giants, built by Beyer Peacock in 1955, hauled 1,200 tonne freight trains between Mombasa on the Indian Ocean and the Kenyan capital of Nairobi. During the 332 mile journey, the line climbs the equivalent of one mile in altitude and the single track route includes 1 in 60 gradients, but the Mountains did the journey in 22 hours with crew changes at Voi and Makindu. The 59s weighed 252 tonnes in full working order and were appropriately named after the highest mountains in East Africa, with such exciting examples as 'Menengai Crater', 'Uluguru Mountains' and 'O' Donya Sabuk'.

PAKISTAN RAILWAYS SPS (2)

4-4-0

The inside cylinder 4-4-0 was the definitive express passenger engine of late Victorian and Edwardian Britain. It was a form of engine prolifically used by most of Britain's pre-grouping railway companies, and examples survived almost until the end of steam. Many of the designs were particularly elegant and graceful. What was once good for Britain was good for the rest of the world too, and the type was exported to India as part of the B.E.S.A. locomotive standardisation programme of 1903. Some SPSs survived until the 1980s, working passenger trains across the dreary plains of the Pakistani Punjab

INDIAN RAILWAYS, BURDWAN TO KATWA

0-6-4T

This is a typical Indian branch line scene on the delightful 2' 6" gauge line from Burdwan to Katwa in Bengal. The engine is No. 3, an 0-6-4T built by Bagnalls of Stafford in 1914. This lovely line was originally worked by McLeod and Co. but became part of India's Eastern Railway in 1966. It is tragic that many of these 2' 6" gauge lines have now closed; they served many communities both urban and rural and provided important feeder services to the main line network. Many succumbed as part of India's rampantly uncontrolled switch from railways to roads.

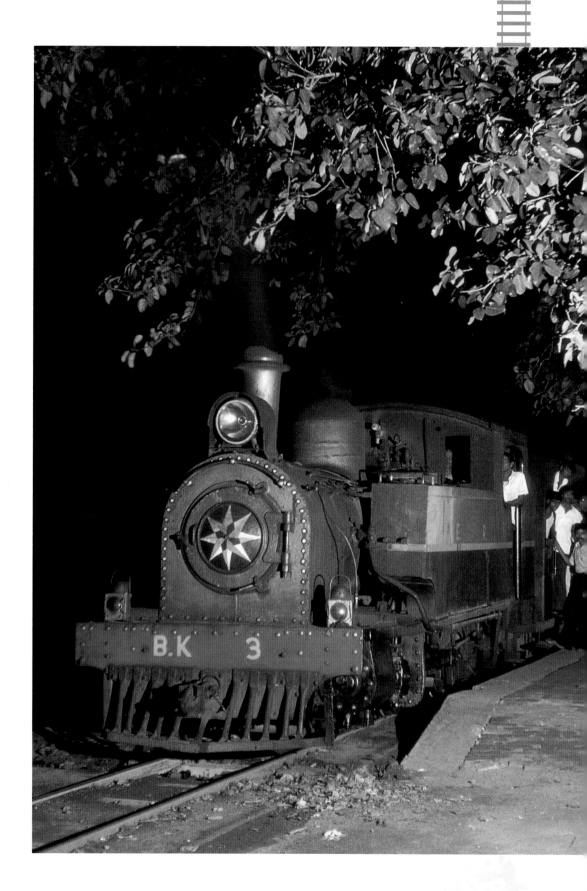

SOUTH AFRICAN RAILWAYS 12A

The British concept of a colliery locomotive was a small saddle tank, but the equivalent in South Africa was invariably a much larger engine to cope with the long distances between the collieries and the main lines and the difficult undulating terrain they often faced. The design of these delightful 12As is derived from the 12 Class heavy mineral engine of 1919. This type was later adapted for colliery service, albeit in un-superheated form, and classified 12A. All came from the North British Works in Glasgow and one, delivered to the Witbank Colliery network, arrived in 1947 in twenty huge wooden packing cases marked 'For the attention of the colliery engineer'.

INDIAN RAILWAYS WT
2-8-4T

The WT Class 2-8-4Ts were the last word in suburban tanks on Indian Railways. The class consisted of thirty locomotives built between 1959 and 1967 at Chittaranjan Locomotive Works. These impressive locomotives had rapid acceleration and were powerful enough to haul heavy trains. Engine No. 14011 was built in 1965 and from its base at Rajamundry, where it is seen taking water, it worked cross-country passenger trains around the Godavri Delta in Andhra Pradesh.

INDIAN RAILWAYS XE
2-8-2

Indian Railway's XE Class 2-8-2s were the largest conventional engines work on the Indian sub-continent. They were introduced in 1928 as part of the X Series Standards with examples coming from the Vulcan Foundry and the legendary Clydeside shipbuilder Beardmore of Dalmuir. The XEs distinguished themselves for almost fifty years hauling 2,000 tonne coal trains over the hill regions of Bengal. Following mass withdrawals during the 1970s, a few were given major overhauls at Jamalpur Works and sold to industrial units where some survived into the 1990s. When the last survivor ended its days at Korba Thermal Power Station in Madhyr Pradesh, it was the last large British steam locomotive left in world service.

CALCUTTA PORT TRUST
0-6-2T

Several generations of British steam locomotives have worked in Calcutta docks but in the later years operations became standardised around these chunky 0-6-2 tanks which first came from Hunslet's works in Leeds in 1945. The Calcutta Port Trust decided to standardise with these locomotives in order to achieve maximum economy of operation. The class totalled 45 engines, later examples coming from the German builder Henschel of Kassel and Mitsubishi of Japan. All were virtually identical in appearance.

INDIAN RAILWAYS INSIDE CYLINDER
0-6-0

The 0-6-0 was the definitive British steam locomotive, and many were grafted onto the Indian sub-continent from all of Britain's leading builders as part of the B.E.S.A. programme of 1904 for standardising designs on India's railways. The type was similar to the Class J11 Pom-Pom of the Great Central Railway, and was widely used as a mixed traffic 'maid of all work'. Originally supplied with saturated boilers, many were later converted to superheaters and classified SGC 2, as is this example phjotographed in Delhi in the 1970s

INDIAN RAILWAYS XD

The 'X Series' Standards, supplied to the Indian sub-continent's 5' 6" gauge railways during the 1920s, consisted primarily of Pacifics and Mikados. The most numerous class in the programme were the XDs which totalled 194 engines. Following their inception in 1929, the design was produced by four different builders. They were superb workhorses, often regarded as superior to the later and more powerful WG Class 2-8-2s. The XDs could work 1,800 tonne coal trains over the 77 miles from Dornakal Junction to Vijayawada in 2½ hours.

ENGINES of WAR

The usefulness of railways in a war zone was first recognized as early as the Crimea Campaign of 1854–56. By the end of World War I, railways were an intrinsic part of warfare with hundreds of miles of narrow gauge tracks leading right up to the front lines. World War II also saw extensive use being made of the rail networks both at home and in the theatre of war. Trains continued to run in the face of increasing attacks from the air as they moved munitions, troops and casualties in the most difficult conditions.

Such was the demand for rail services at home and abroad that intensive locomotive building programmes were set up by all the participants to feed the war effort. Engines from the U.S.A. were sent all around the world to support the United States Army Transportation Corps. 'Austerity' types appeared, quick to build and easy to maintain, whilst the Third Reich's workhorse of World War II was the 2-10-0 'Kreigslokomotive' which was produced in several guises, with over 6,000 examples of one type alone being produced between 1943 and the end of the war. Many of these engines of war lingered on in their adopted countries long after the end of hostilities, continuing to give excellent service.

U.S.A. NO. 30067

0-6-0T

American mass-production techniques were called on to build locomotives quickly for service during World War II. Two of their smaller manufacturers, Vulcan and Porter, produced no fewer than 438 six-coupled shunting tanks for shipment to Europe in 1942–43 and the engines were stored in Britain until required on the continent. At the end of the war, many remained unused, still in store at dumps around the country. A group of the engines stored at Newbury were inspected by Bulleid in 1946 and subsequently purchased by the Southern Railway for use in Southampton Docks.

L.N.E.R. J94

0-6-0ST

World War II brought a new customer for the Hunslet 18' saddletank – the British War Department, who urgently needed shunting locomotives for military use. The Hunslet design was preferred above the L.M.S. 3F 0-6-0T for this role, and no fewer than 377 were turned out by seven different builders after 1943. At the end of the war, the L.N.E.R. bought 75 of the engines to become their class J94 and scattered them widely round their docks and goods yards. But their finest moment came in B.R. days when they were deployed on the tortuous curves and gradients of the Cromford & High Peak line in Derbyshire.

W.D. 'AUSTERITY'

2-8-0

By 1943, the demand for heavy freight engines to assist the war effort was exceeding supply. The excellent L.M.S. Stanier 8F 2-8-0 was proving too expensive in materials and too time-consuming in construction, so a more economical solution was sought. In designing the W.D. 2-8-0, Robert Riddles took every opportunity to make the locomotive cheaper and quicker to manufacture. A parallel boiler with round-topped firebox replaced the Belpaire taper boiler of the 8F, whilst steel castings and forgings were eliminated by the use of fabricated components and all other parts were kept as simple as possible.

U.S.A. TC

0-6-0T

The Southern Railway took 14 of the U.S.A. TC tanks into stock in 1947. To British eyes, their all-American appearance with features such as bar frames, boiler-top sandboxes and stovepipe chimneys made them look a little outlandish, but they were soon Anglicised with improved cabs, extended coal bunkers and British-style regulator handles. Their short wheelbase made them ideal for dock shunting work, and they put in years of useful work at Southampton. Two were painted in Southern green livery and one of these, B.R. No. 30064, was a popular choice for preservation and now operates on the Bluebell Railway in Sussex.

ROW OF W.D. 'AUSTERITIES'

2-8-0s

In all, around 900 W.D. 2-8-0s were built in a period of three years. After the war, 200 of them were taken into L.N.E.R. stock in 1946 and others were disposed of abroad. Eventually no fewer than 733 came into the possession of British Railways in 1948. They slogged on, grimy and neglected, until the 1960s, but in the end every single one went for scrap. However, one locomotive that had worked in Holland and been sold in 1952 to the Swedish State Railways was discovered near the Arctic Circle and brought back to work on the Worth Valley Railway.

G.C.R. O4

2-8-0

In 1941, the call to arms came again for the Robinson O4 class 2-8-0s and the War Department despatched 92 of them to the Middle East. Some of these were the same engines that had been requisitioned in 1917, but this time they did not return home. After World War II, those that remained on the L.N.E.R. were generally confined to ex-G.C.R. routes and withdrawals began in 1958. The class was extinct by 1966, with the notable exception of No. 63601 which was set aside for the National Collection and has since been restored to working order.

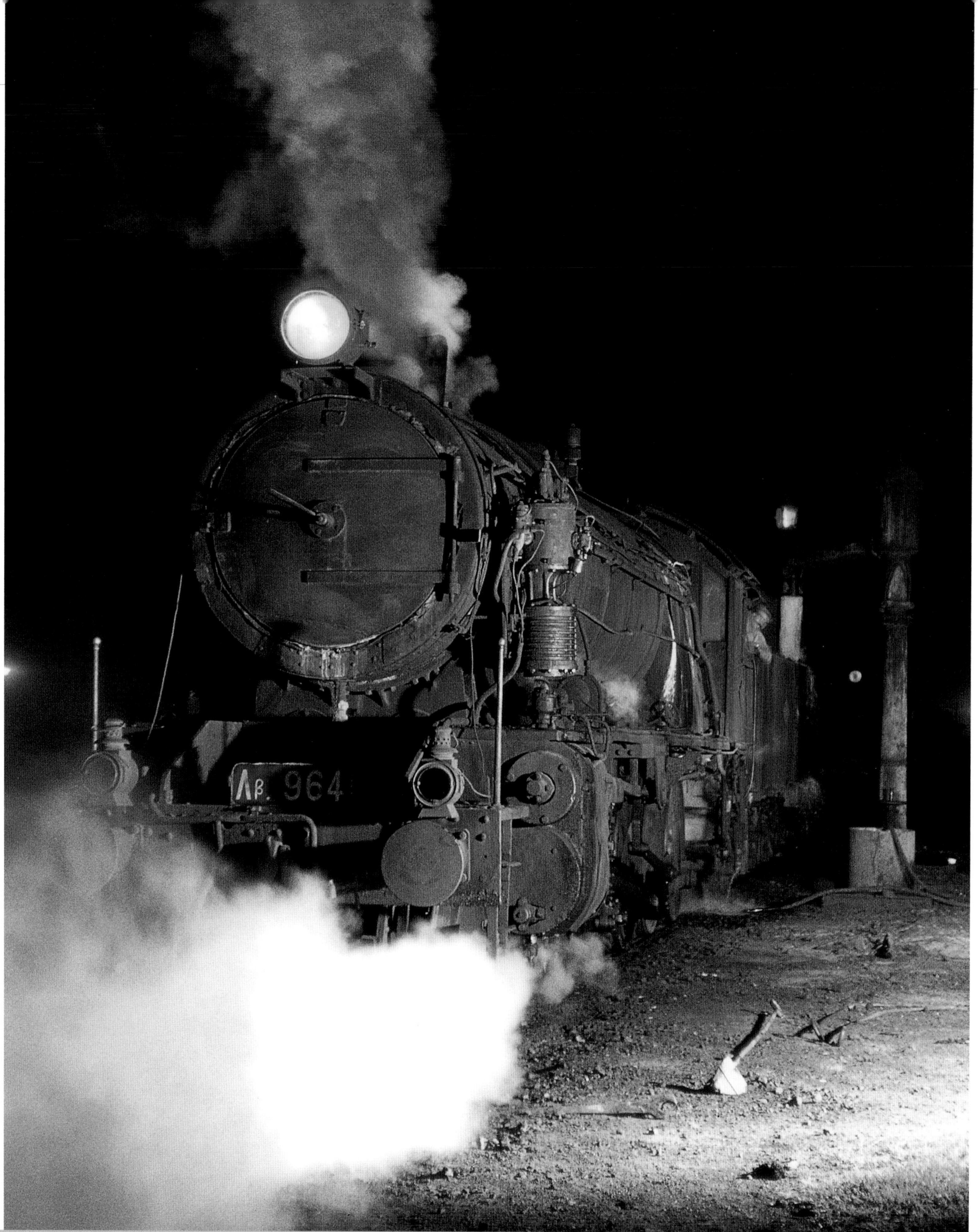
Λβ 964

W.D.

2-10-0

Having produced an excellent 2-8-0 for wartime service, Robert Riddles considered that a larger version would be desirable and expanded the design into a 2-10-0. Its great advantage was its bigger boiler with a wide firebox, allowing it to steam well on poor quality coal. 150 locomotives were built by North British in Glasgow, the first appearing in 1943, and many saw service on the L.M.S. and L.N.E.R. before being shipped abroad. Some were sent on to Egypt and Syria and remained there after the war. The Egyptian contingent was later transferred to the Hellenic Railways of Greece where they put in a further 28 years of work.

W.D. 'AUSTERITY'

2-8-0

Monochrome photography is somehow appropriate to record a filthy, work-stained W.D. 2-8-0. Consigned to the hardest and least glamorous work on the railway in the industrial northeast, they slaved on in considerable numbers until displaced by B.R. Standard 9F 2-10-0s in the 1950s. No. 90459 is captured in characteristic grimy condition, filling up before its next turn of duty from an elegant North Eastern Railway water crane.

W.D.
2-10-0

By far the largest group of W.D. 2-10-0s congregated in Holland where some continued working until the mid-1950s. One of these, the historic 1000th war engine, is on display in the Utrecht Railway Museum. At the end of the war, Britain's railways were less enthusiastic about adopting the returning W.D. 2-10-0s and preferred the eight-coupled version. Nevertheless, B.R. did take 25 of the class into stock as Nos. 90750–74. Several locomotives were retained by the Army, and the last of these, No. 600 'Gordon', can be seen on the Severn Valley Railway. Two of the Hellenic Railways locomotives have been repatriated to the North Yorkshire Moors Railway where W.D. No.73672 has been named 'Dame Vera Lynn'.

W.D. 'AUSTERITY'
2-8-0

Special attention was paid to making the W.D. 2-8-0 adaptable to the altered conditions of war service, so the boiler could quickly be converted for oil-firing without its removal from the engine. On the tender, the narrow coal bunker gave good rearward visibility when the engine was working tender first, as it often had to do. The class immediately went into volume production by North British and Vulcan Foundry in 1943 and proved very successful in many spheres of operation, first in Britain before D-Day, and then in France, Belgium, Holland and further afield.

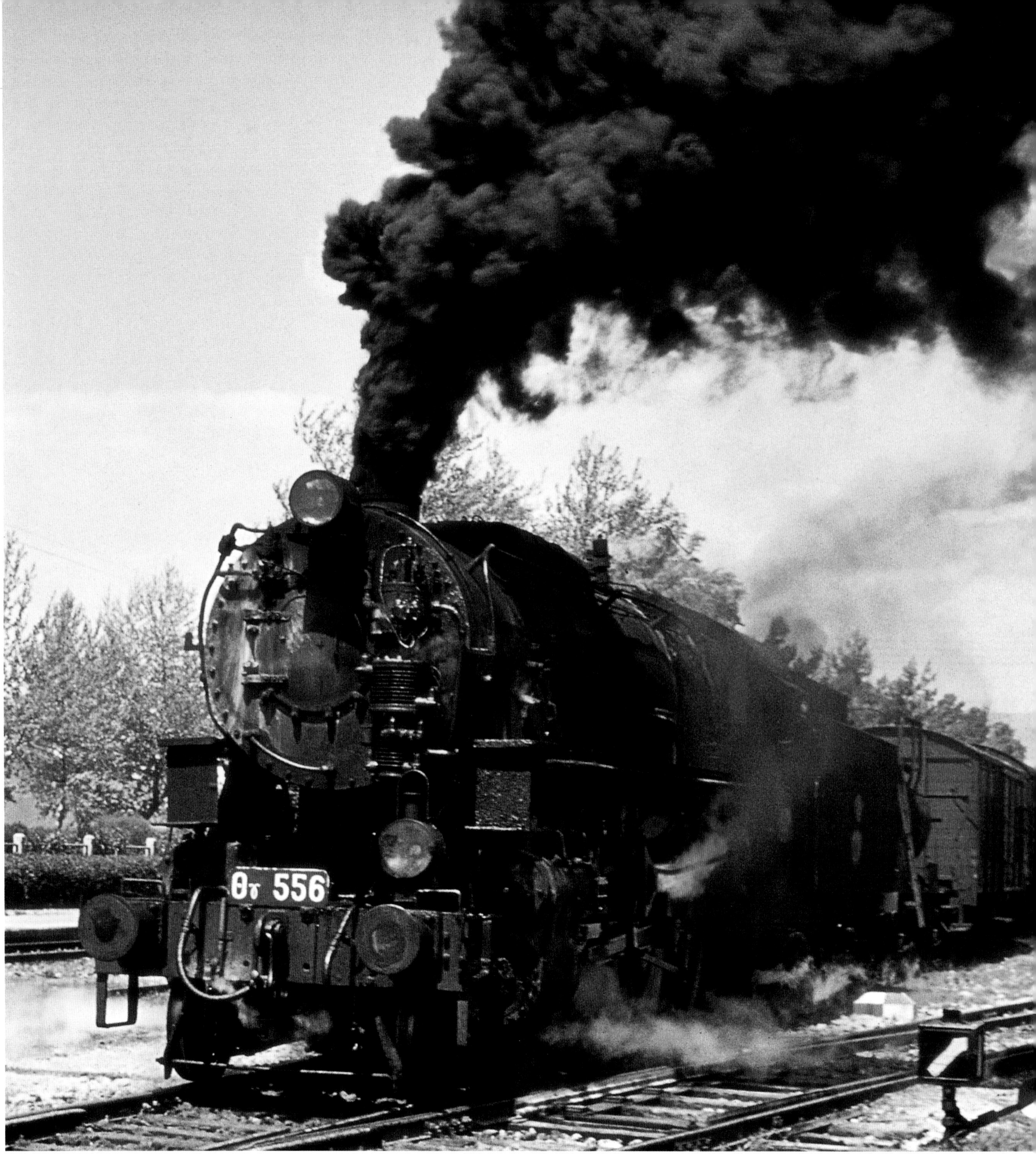
Θγ 556

S160 WORKING IN GREECE

2-8-0

The same specification as for the Riddles W.D. 'Austerities' was laid down by the British Ministry of Supply for the American S160 class 2-8-0s, the only proviso being that they should conform to the British loading gauge. A design team headed by Major J. W. Marsh drew up a locomotive that could be built quickly and in large numbers by the big three U.S. builders, Alco, Baldwin and Lima, making use of standard parts. Over 800 of the class actually operated in Britain before being shipped to the war zone. Many stayed in Europe after the conflict and some fifty engines ran in Greece until the 1970s.

SUDAN RAILWAYS '220'

4-6-2

Sudan's most numerous locomotive type were the '220' class Pacifics. First built in 1927, a total of 51 engines had come from North British by 1947 and the design was adopted as a standard by the British War Department, examples later being constructed for the Nyasaland and Trans-Zambesia Railways, as well as the Western Australian Railways. In later years, these engines worked turn-about with the related '180' and '310' class Mikados, the last of which entered service in 1952. All three classes used the same boiler and other standard interchangeable parts.

INDUSTRIAL LOCOMOTIVES

It is appropriate that the industrial locomotive, the first category of locomotive to be built, should be the last to go. All the developments in those first few years of steam trains were geared around the use of steam in an industrial environment. Long after steam had vanished from the main lines of Britain, an army of small engines – invariably 0-4-0s and 0-6-0s – could be found hard at work in power stations, quarries, coal mines and docks.

To properly fulfil its role, the industrial engine needed to be compact and economical, able to work over temporary track, negotiate tight curves and yet have sufficient adhesion to be able to draw heavy trainloads of earth and other materials. Additionally, the engines had to be easy to transport from one site to another. Small tank engines met all these requirements.

Industrial engines were always associated with the towns in which their builders were located: Andrew Barclay in Kilmarnock; Robert Stephenson and Hawthorn Leslie both in Newcastle-upon-Tyne; and William Bagnall in Stafford, to name but a few. In Leeds, in the tiny parish of Hunslet, there were four celebrated builders: Manning Wardle, Hudswell Clarke, Kitsons and Hunslet. These engines preceded their main line counterparts by some twenty years, and survived them by approximately the same margin.

BAGNALL 'ENTERPRISE' AT PRESTON DOCKS

0-6-0ST

Bagnalls of Stafford were one of the foremost industrial locomotive builders in Britain, and over the years developed a range of useful and attractive machines in a variety of sizes suited to the needs of industrial users. In 1934 they produced the first of a class of powerful 16'-cylindered 0-6-0 saddletanks which found favour with collieries in their native Staffordshire as well as being supplied to Preston Docks Authority. Here, one of the Preston engines, 'Enterprise', gets to grips with a heavy train on the dockside.

R.S.H. AT LEICESTER POWER STATION

0-4-0ST

Although built by Robert Stephenson & Hawthorns of Newcastle as recently as 1950, this smart little locomotive bears all the design hallmarks of their predecessors, Hawthorn Leslie & Co., being one of their standard four-coupled 12' saddletanks, a design produced without significant alteration over a period of 40 years. The type found great favour within the electricity generating industry, and many power stations including that at Leicester depicted here relied on their capacity for hard work until the advent of 'merry-go-round' train operation.

HUNSLET 16' AT NASSINGTON QUARRY

0-6-0STs

In 1923 the Hunslet Engine Company produced the first of their useful 16' cylinder class, which was destined to be built in considerable numbers over the next 35 years. The delightfully named pair, 'Ring Haw' and 'Jacks Green', were supplied to the ironstone quarries at Nassington when this modern system opened in 1939 and spent their entire working lives there. Always well maintained, both engines were bought for preservation when the quarry closed, 'Ring Haw' going to the North Norfolk Railway and her sister to the Nene Valley Railway near Peterborough.

HUNSLET 16'

0-6-0ST

At the ironstone quarries of the East Midlands, the golden ore scooped up by the Ruston-Bucyrus steam excavator was loaded directly into standard gauge wagons running over temporary tracks at the very lip of the quarry. Here at Nassington quarry, the two Hunslet 16' saddletanks, 'Jacks Green' and 'Ring Haw' wait patiently for this operation to be completed before blasting their way up the steep gradients to the main line interchange sidings.

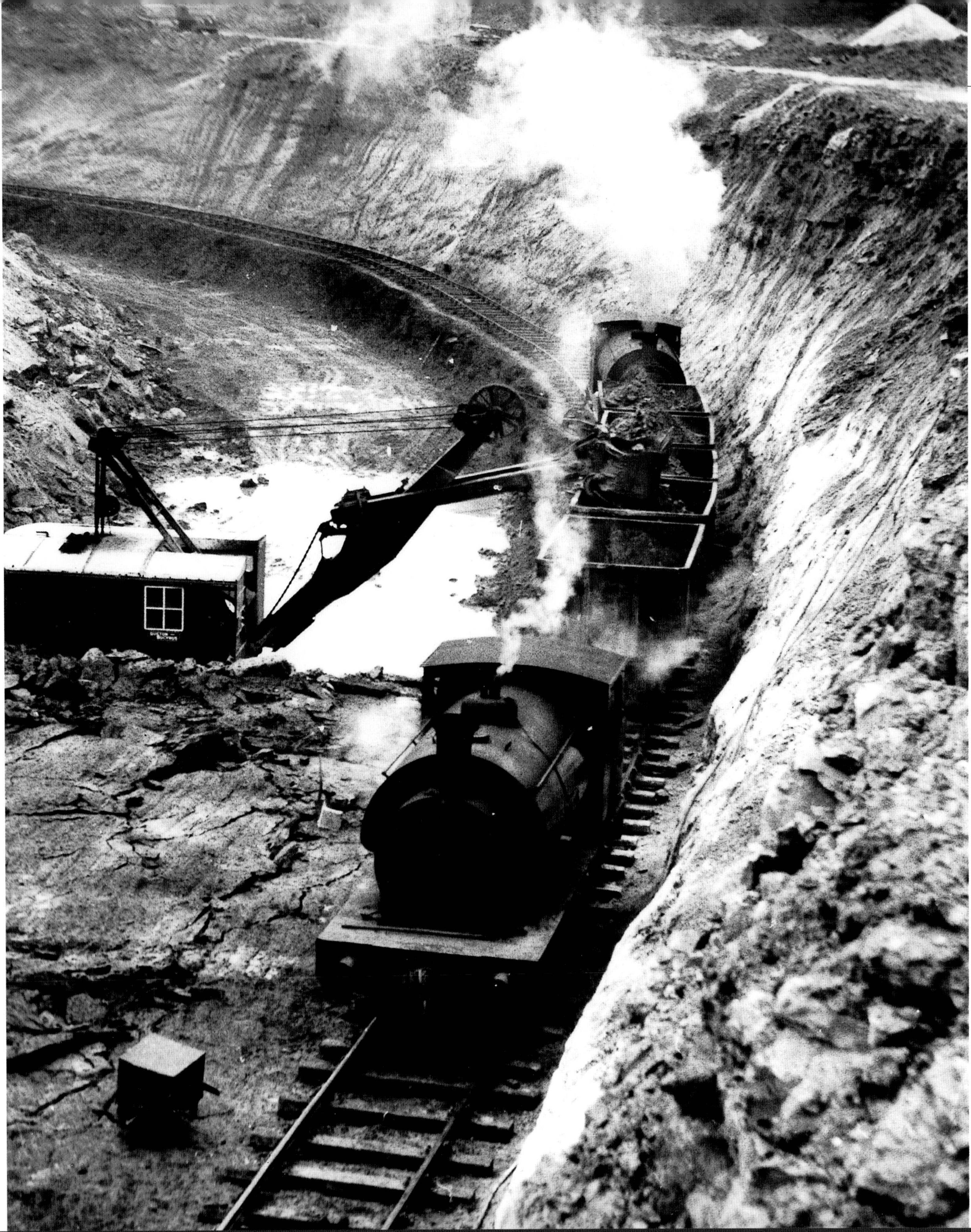

R.S.H. 16' 'PROGRESS'
0-6-0ST

When Robert Stephenson & Co. merged with Hawthorn Leslie in 1937, the new R.S.H. company perpetuated many of the attractive Hawthorn Leslie industrial locomotive designs, many of them dating back before World War I. Such an engine is 'Progress', built at Newcastle in 1946 for colliery service in Leicestershire, first at Moira, then Measham and finally at Cadley Hill, where she was maintained in first class condition until the end of steam operations there.

G.W.R. 57XX
0-6-0PT

The National Coal Board were quick to appreciate the usefulness of the G.W.R. 57XX pannier tanks when they started becoming surplus to Western Region requirements. They were versatile, free-running machines and generated remarkable power at low speeds – all good attributes for an industrial locomotive and especially valuable in the collieries of the south Wales valleys where these Swindon cast-offs were deployed. No. 7754 served successfully at Mountain Ash Colliery until bought for preservation on the Llangollen Railway.

ANDREW BARCLAY AT GOLDINGTON
0-4-0ST

Best-known of the Scottish industrial locomotive builders, Andrew Barclay of Kilmarnock began manufacture in 1859. Their locomotives gained a reputation for toughness and hard work, virtues embodied in their popular 14' saddletanks. Two of these were delivered new to Goldington Power Station in Bedfordshire in 1954, but were soon converted by the manufacturers to oil-burning. The reliability and economy achieved by the conversion kept both locomotives regularly employed at the power station for quarter of a century.

HUNSLET 'AUSTERITY'
0-6-0ST

Another significant customer for the war surplus 'Austerity' saddletanks was the newly-formed National Coal Board, who bought 47 and found them so useful that they promptly ordered more from Hunslets. Further industrial customers also adopted the design until the 'Austerity' had become the most numerous steam locomotive in industrial service in Britain. Hunslet continued construction up to 1964, when the final pair of locomotives were delivered to the N.C.B. Over the years, several of the type have benefited from such aids to efficiency and economy as Giesl ejectors, producer gas fuelling and underfeed stokers.

HUDSWELL CLARKE AT DESFORD COLLIERY

0-6-0ST

The family of inside-cylindered 0-6-0 saddletanks produced by the three Leeds manufacturers, Manning Wardle, Hunslet and Hudswell Clarke, could all trace their ancestry back to the designs of E. B. Wilson's Railway Foundry. They were the staple workhorses of British industry for more than a century, serving quarries, iron and steel works, coal mines and a whole host of other manufacturing industries. In this timeless scene at Desford Colliery in Leicestershire, a classic Hudswell Clarke is hard at work against a backdrop of pithead winding gear.

HUNSLET 18' 'AUSTERITY'

0-6-0ST

The industrial locomotive design produced in greatest numbers was without doubt the 'Austerity' 0-6-0ST. Its origin can be found in the Hunslet 18' saddletank, which with slight modification was chosen as the standard shunting locomotive for the Ministry of Supply in World War II. As well as the ex-W.D. engines sold to the L.N.E.R., the National Coal Board bought 47 and were so impressed that they immediately ordered a new batch from Hunslet. Eventually 234 locomotives were in N.C.B. service.

N.C.B. ANDREW BARCLAY

0-6-0ST

Andrew Barclay, Sons & Co. of Kilmarnock began building steam locomotives in 1859 and continued to produce sturdy and reliable machines, mostly for industrial use, for the next 100 years before turning to the manufacture of diesel shunters and railcars. Unmistakable Barclay features such as the flat-sided saddletank extending over the smokebox and the thick, chunky wheel centres and spokes distinguish their appearance, whilst the earlier locomotives featured attractive curved cab sheeting. Such a locomotive was Barclay 0-6-0ST No. 1015 of 1904, seen here hard at work at Shotton Colliey, County Durham.

DOXFORD CRANE TANK

0-4-0

Crane tanks were never numerous on British main line railways, but found a specialist niche in industrial use. The family of Hawthorn Leslie and Robert Stephenson & Hawthorns 0-4-0 crane tanks employed at Doxford's Pallion shipyard in Sunderland were ideal machines for carrying heavy shipbuilding components around the dockside. When not in use, the crane jib rested on the locomotive's chimney, but by regulating the steam supply to the lifting cylinder, the jib could be raised. A separate two-cylinder engine mounted on top of the unique T-shaped boiler could slew the jib round through 360 degrees, allowing loads of up to four tonnes to be swung into position.

BEWARE OF ENGINES

R.S.H. BACKWORTH COLLIERY 18'

0-6-0ST

These powerful 18' saddletanks began to appear in significant numbers on the colliery lines in their native northeast in the 1950s, and the type played an important part on the N.C.B. systems at Philadelphia and Ashington in the latter days of industrial steam. The type was popular with engine crews who appreciated their abundance of power and large, roomy cabs. Although this particular example from Backworth Colliery did not survive the demise of the coal industry, other fine examples of the breed have found a home on the Tanfield Railway on Tyneside.

ANDREW BARCLAY 16' AT DALMELLINGTON

0-4-0ST

The Andrew Barclay 0-4-0 saddletanks on the Dalmellington system were the company's standard 16' product but when working hard on the run to Pennyvenie Colliery they could consume up to two tons of coal per shift – well in excess of the amount that could be carried on the footplate. Accordingly, they were each paired with an improvised tender made from a cut-down colliery wagon. This was a feature of operations on the N.C.B. Waterside system for many years and the six tonne capacity of these tenders enabled the engines to work for several days without re-coaling.

KITSON (MW-TYPE WITH BARCLAY)

0-6-0ST

The ironstone railways of Northamptonshire were a happy hunting ground for enthusiasts in search of industrial locomotives at work in delightful rural surroundings. Although they served the process of opencast ironstone quarrying, their character was far removed from the grime and clangour of heavy industry. The railway at Storefield, for instance, ran through leafy woodland amid attractive rolling countryside. Its stud of Barclay 0-4-0STs were joined latterly by the Kitson 0-6-0ST 'Caerphilly', a locomotive whose design can be credited to the famous Leeds builders, Manning Wardle & Co.

BEYER PEACOCK
GARRATT

0-4-4-0T

Beyer Peacock & Co. will best be remembered for their matchless Garratt articulated designs supplied to railways across the world. Apart from those they built for the L.M.S. and L.N.E.R. companies, Beyer Peacock also constructed four Garratts for industrial firms in Britain. The last survivor was 'William Francis', which was delivered new to Baddesley Colliery in Warwickshire and remained there throughout its working life. On withdrawal, it was fittingly set aside for preservation and may now be seen at Bressingham Steam Museum in Norfolk.

R.S.H. AT CASTLE DONINGTON

0-4-0ST

Hawthorn Leslie and their successors, Robert Stephenson & Hawthorns, developed a range of powerful four-coupled locomotives that combined a high tractive effort with the flexibility of a short wheelbase. Castle Donington power station employed a pair of R.S.H. 0-4-0STs for internal shunting when it started generating in 1956. They were always maintained in excellent condition and their 16' cylinders were needed to apply the necessary power for moving trains of loaded coal hopper wagons from the exchange sidings to the wagon tippler.

ANDREW BARCLAY NO. 17

0-6-0T

This handsome 18' 0-6-0T was supplied new in 1913 by Andrew Barclay of Kilmarnock to the Dalmellington Ironworks Company in Ayrshire for hauling coal traffic from Pennyvenie Colliery, some 3½ miles away. No. 17 had a remarkable 60 year career on the steeply-graded line – no other British industrial locomotive had so long a continuous working life over one route. After the ironworks closed, the collieries remained in operation, eventually becoming incorporated into the N.C.B.'s West Ayr Area, and No. 17 received a thorough overhaul as late as 1971. When the system finally closed, enthusiasts could not bear to see such a fine locomotive go for scrap and she has been preserved on the Tanfield Railway in County Durham.

INDEX